I AM NOT YOUR AVERAGE TEEN

I AM NOT YOUR AVERAGE TEEN

From silence to happiness:
The journey to find my voice

Brittany Krystantos

Copyright © 2016 by Brittany Krystantos
All rights reserved. No part of this book may be reproduced or transmitted in any forms or any means, electronic, recorded, printed, without written permission from the author: Brittany Krystantos.

Front and back cover design by Ivana Carlosena
www.carlosenamedia.com

Website created by Felipe Gabriele
www.rebrandnew.com

Formatted by Theresa McNeilly
www.theresamcneilly.com

Photography by Stephanie Xu

Publication date: March 8, 2016
Printed by CreateSpace
ISBN-13: 978-1512330076
ISBN-10: 1512330078

To order a copy of "I Am Not Your Average Teen" visit: www.brittkrystantos.com

This book is dedicated to the people who push past obstacles like dusting off a fly, continue life even when they wish there was a stop button. You are warriors. Thank you for going beyond your limits. I'd like to acknowledge the teens who couldn't find the strength within them to keep fighting this struggle that is called life. To those who ended their lives too early. I dedicate this book to you in heaven, hopefully pulling forces up there to help me be the best leader, friend, mentor I can possibly be for teens today.
To all teenagers:
This is for you.
♡

Contents

FOREWORD	8
INTRODUCTION	19
ABOUT THE BOOK	20
MY BECOMING	23
THE AWAKENING	25
THE GIFT	28
TOOLS	30
HAVE YOU EVER FELT LIKE THIS?	32
TWELVE SPIRITUAL CONCEPTS	189
MESSAGE FROM MY MENTORS	210
DEAR ALL MY READERS	211
ACKNOWLEDGMENTS	212
ABOUT THE AUTHOR	220

Chapters

1 Brave.................................... 34

2 The Social Struggle...................... 46

3 Be Fearless.............................. 61

4 Life..................................... 69

5 Worth.................................... 74

6 Healing.................................. 82

7 Belonging................................ 97

8 Infinite Possibilities

   Inspired by my Grandfather: Zaida Lorrie............ 108

9 Perception............................... 112

10 Imperfection............................ 120

11 Kindness................................ 127

12 Trust................................... 131

13 Love Yourself........................... 139

14 Yoga

   The dance of my life by: Paria Mirazimi 149

15 Divine Timing........................... 159

16 Her Evil Reflection..................... 162

17 I See You

   A collective group of brave, honest beautiful people, inspiring teens and adults that share their story 170

18 Being Average Sucks..................... 206

Foreword

I remember the first day I met Brittany. I was at a charitable event called Motionball. This is a day for playing a variety of sports with Special Olympics athletes. It supports the Toronto Sick Children's Hospital. Brittany's dad, Mitch, volunteers at the hospital. He spends time with children who are suffering from cancer. Brittany has obviously inherited her dad's love, support and caring nature.

I first saw Britt as a pleasant, wholesome, and SHY teen.

When I got to know her, I realized she is like an angel.

The Merriam-Webster Dictionary defines an angel like this:

1. A spiritual being who serves, especially as a messenger from God, or as a guardian of human beings
2. A person (such as a child) who is very good, kind, beautiful, etc.

This is Brittany. She is a servant of God and the universe.
On the day we met, there were about 10 players on our team. One was the young actor and sports superstar, Luke Bilyk, his sister, Christina Bilyk, and their parents. Luke played Drew Torres on Degrassi.

The universe has a way of revealing things to Britt at exactly the right time. My daughter, Mikayla, came with me to the games, and she and Britt became instant friends.

Britt seems to have a sixth sense. She feels things, loves, and cares deeply and expresses herself eloquently. She seems to have a unique ability to understand people, events and things beyond normal human understanding and intellect. It's almost as if she possesses a certain "knowing" about people and things. I'm not sure if you'd say she has Extrasensory Perception (ESP), but when you read her story, you have to wonder. When she was a mute child, when she didn't have language, she had to feel things and express herself with her own energy, body language and eye contact.

When Motionball was over, I wanted to stay in contact with Brittany. I was drawn to her as most people are. She is the same age as my daughter, and I felt a very strong connection to this bright, curious child – this blossoming angel.

After a few conversations back and forth, I invited Britt out to a TV show where she, my son, Brandon, and my daughter were modelling some sports clothing. The idea was to demonstrate activities that kids can do to have fun and stay active.

Britt's and my friendship deepened shortly afterwards. We went out together several times, and I discovered her desire to write. She was full of so many things to say. It was as if her brain didn't stop, and as if the voices in her head were louder than the ones in real life. She was compelled to share, help, inspire.

I introduced her to my business partner and webmaster, Patrick Binetti, founder of Build a Blog School. I suggested that Britt start her own blog. She was 15. Patrick helped her to launch www.brittlives2inspire.com.

One of Brittany's posts reached more than 1600 views and shares on Facebook alone. People loved her message and praised her for her authenticity.

I have witnessed her physical, mental, emotional and intellectual growth. She has transformed her body into a healthy, lean machine from a softer, fuller version of herself. She seemed to shed away her "baby fat" to unravel the goddess she is today. She was always there. She has just taken on a new form. It is a sign of her values to be stronger, healthier and pure in every way.

Her writing has taken on a mature form as she has grown. She expresses herself unapologetically and with immense clarity. She knows what she wants to say and when to say it. It impacts those who need to hear it.

I have been inspired by her many times. I have had the privilege of meeting some of the world's great influencers and leaders of thought. I believe that Brittany is among these people and on her way to a greatness the world may not even be prepared for.

I have watched how people light up when they're around her. They seem inspired to be with her. She brings out the best in people by challenging their thoughts and way of being. This eternally inquisitive person questions you. She asks you to be introspective, to reflect and acknowledge the actions, people and circumstances that do not serve you.

Britt is a force of nature who ignites and sparks our inner drives, challenges our fears and urges us to break loose of anything holding us back from being our most powerful and loving selves.

It has been an honor and a pleasure to be part of her journey, to witness her growth and to share in her family's pride of her. I love her and wish her all the best, because she deserves all the credit in the world. I'm glad I was able to point her to a platform so the world can experience this living angel.

Brittany, you do "live 2 inspire", and I am looking forward to seeing what's next on your journey.

Carmelia Ray
Well-known Toronto author, speaker, dating, matchmaking & attraction expert

I choose to speak my truth
. . .

Let's begin

the journey.

I AM NOT YOUR AVERAGE TEEN

The Journey To

14

Find My Voice

I AM NOT YOUR AVERAGE TEEN

This is who I am

My world:

Welcome to it.

Join me with an open mind.

Leave your ego behind.

Let's journey together to find our truest selves:

behind the lies, behind false hopes.

This is my journey: from silence to happiness.

To find my voice.

There has been a lot of searching.

A lot of wonder.

Who am I, Universe?

My truth was blinded

By the world bringing me down.

My teachers said one thing.

My parents said another.

My peers said another.

The world said another.

One day I took off my blindfolds.

I saw the truth, and it set me free.

I was counting the days until high school finished

And the real world started.

Popularity, once my quest,

Finding myself, my only mission,

Fighting darkness; slaying demons,

Standing tall,

Day by day; moment to moment; little by little.

Walking my discovery,

Walking my journey,

To love myself;

To speak my truth;

To heal my past;

To know myself fully;

To feel my confidence;

To root myself, and stand my ground,

Making a mark on this world.

This is who I am.

Curious youth to motivated woman.

~
Britt Krystantos

Dear Young Brittany,
2014. 14 years old.

Thank you for not giving up when things looked their worst. That night when you thought about what the world would be like without you? You were so close to following through. I'm so grateful you chose life, no matter what it was that stopped you. I know you experienced life feeling empty and lonely, and that you suffered silently.

I know you felt as though nobody understood you and as if you had no real friends. I know you felt like an outcast. I remember when your friends laughed at you. I remember when people wrote "dumb blonde" on that anonymous site. When you saw those hurtful words, you started to believe them, didn't you?

What you didn't know then is that life is awesome, and there is so much to be excited about. You were never alone. Life is a journey. Sometimes things don't make sense. Sometimes life seems unfair.

There's a purpose for everything; even the most painful experiences have helped you grow into the person you are today. Your tears of pain are now tears of joy, aren't they? You couldn't see then what you now understand. Those difficult times were just a part of the journey.

You're gone now, in the past, where all you ever wanted was to feel loved and like you mattered. While I continue life, heading to my future; I will always remember you, as the girl who is strong. You gave me strength. You gave me hope. You gave me life. You gave me everything I needed, in order to be who I am today.

When you realized that there are still more snowflakes to see, more people to meet, more places to visit — when you realized there is a whole world waiting for you, it was the best decision you ever made.

You continued to follow the road. I love you forever and always.

Sincerely,
New Britt

Introduction

Hi there. I'm Brittany, but I prefer that you call me Britt.

In the seventeen years I've been alive, there's one major thing I've come to realize, and that is we are constantly rediscovering ourselves. We change and evolve as we hit storms that challenge us and define who we are.

But guess what? All these ups and downs uncover the one thing that we all want to know. Am I settling to be someone I am not, or is this who I really am?

I've come to terms with the fact that we're all different and there's no shame in living your life the way you want. I am me and I am perfect just the way I am. Just like you're perfect, just the way you are! This is me, you are you – all different but awesome in our own unique ways.

People always tell me, "Brittany, you're not the 'average' teen". The adults always seem to be the ones who like the fact that I don't attend high school parties. The teens disagree, and find it's 'weird'.

Does that automatically make me a loser?

About The Book

Yay! Somehow you found this book. Maybe you found it on the road and it's dirty and dusty. Who knows? Maybe your friend gave it to you. Or you heard about it and went to the store to buy it. I see it like this, one way or another, you're meant to receive this book. It's time to answer the questions you have about yourself: Who am I?

Whatever way this book landed in the palms of your hands, I thank you. I'm grateful that you're reading the story of my young view on life and how I created tools to help bring me to a brighter world versus the one I was living before my discovery. I'm beyond happy to be a part of your transformation.

Get ready! *This is my world and I welcome you* to it with arms wide open. I am not a preacher. I will never force you into doing anything you're not comfortable with. You always have a choice.

I won't be physically there to walk to school with you. I won't be there to hangout with you in your house, after school or on the weekend. My voice will be with you at all times.

Remember, I'm just a book away.

If you ever need an image of what I look like to remind yourself that I am here for you throughout this journey, then create me in your mind. See me as a girl with blue eyes and long blonde hair. I am 5'1" tall.

See me speaking to you, telling you these exact words: *"You, my friend, can get through any, and I mean ANY, obstacle."*

If you already understand that we all have the strength within us to be who we are, then you are ready to use that knowledge to acquire the tools necessary for self- realization.

When someone once said to me, "Let me guide you, teach you, and mentor you", I instantly got defensive and said: "What – do you think I have a problem?"

You don't have any issues that need to be fixed. This isn't about fixing you, or making you someone else, because you're awesome just the way you are. This is about discovering new activities, tools, and things that can help you live a happier life. Isn't that what you want?

If you do know who you really are, and you're confident with the person you are, great. This will be easy for you. If life ever gets really hard and you start to forget who you are, all you do is look at this book as a reminder to bring you one step back to the real person that you've once known.

There's not one person in this world who doesn't deserve to be happy. Who wouldn't want to find ways to be better than who they were yesterday? Half the time you might be used to being told you're not good enough. Maybe this feeling has become your constant thought, your constant reminder. And maybe your constant response is: "What – you think I need help? Am I not good enough for you?" We're human. We all think it. I did, too.

Before we dive into deep, deep stuff, let me share with you my vision for this book. I've gotten many questions like, *"why do you write?"*

The only answer that comes out of my mouth is I do it for **YOU** teens, the ones who have gotten lost on your way of becoming young adults.

Like you, there was a time when I thought life was just about surrounding myself with "the popular people at school", partying and looking cool. However, there is much more then that. I thought I was a person I wasn't.

Through this book I will share how the tools through my experience helped me get to where I am today, as a new me. The words that kept me motivated were "**You can do it**". I know you can do it, that you will make it through whatever rainy or snowy storm that has come your way.

Sometimes the only words that we manage to get out of our mouths are "life sucks", and that's okay. Often I get annoyed with the saying, "At the end of the tunnel there is light", but it's true. There will always be darkness, but there is always light, too, so crawl and escape from any darkness that keeps sucking you in. The light is waiting patiently for you.

I encourage you to take your time. We can't discover who we are in just one minute. Can you imagine if we were able to do that? So many people would have their lives all figured out without any challenges. Life wouldn't be a struggle anymore, and nobody would find it hard to make it to the next day.

Someone once asked me: "What do you do when life falls apart?" And my answer is this: There's nowhere to run, like the way you would in a game of tag in second grade. It's about letting yourself feel the pain, the grief, the resentment you have for yourself, the anger for your family. And the confusion you have about who you really are.

You can make it your intention to 'just be', like 'living with the flow of the sea', just being, with no expectations.

I would love to stay connected. My readers are my reason for writing. If something seems 'dope' or in other words, inspirational to you, than share it. If you ever feel inspired during this journey, Tweet, Instagram or Facebook me, by doing two things: tag and hashtag. @Brittkrystantos #WhoWants2BeUrAverageTeen

With this book, I will be whatever you want me to be, your inner voice, your friend, your mentor or your leader.

I Love you all,

Britt Krystantos

My Becoming

Three years ago

It's my first year of high school. It's been four months, and I have no clue who I am. I thought I knew it all. I have my six friends, I'm in a popular group, and when people think of my name, "Brittany Krystantos", they think of me as "the popular blonde girl" who's beyond perfect.

Am I, though? The bell rings for third period lunch. I walk downstairs to the atrium, where my friends are all standing. I'm surrounded by hot grade ten boys, and I keep wondering: Is this who I am?

I stand in the middle of the atrium. I see my friend from middle school who has always been there for me. (She sat beside me in "stupid sped class", because we were both told: "You're a little slower than our average students." Who wants to be classified as a '100 percent student' anyways? I'm done trying to be an academic student.

Should I go over to her and eat lunch with her today? No, that'll make me look like a loser.

I see my old friend. I've known him for 14 years. He was my first "forever friend". Maybe I should eat lunch with him?

Perhaps I should just eat my lunch with the cool girls. It'll remain my spot at the "popular" table. But if I go up to them right now, and right away, they will think I am desperate, so I better wait a few minutes.

All of us ninth graders from *Westmount Collegiate Institute* are still socializing in the atrium, talking rather than eating our lunches.

This is high school for you: We have the jocks; the cheerleaders/dancers; the stoners; the "wannabes"; the goths; the hockey stars; the ones who spend their weekends watching "The Walking Dead"; the nerds; the losers; the weirdos.

Then there is me. I am the one who is incredibly confused about who I am. I have entered high school thinking that fitting in will be easy. I thought my blonde hair and fashionable clothes would hasten this experience.

I was wrong.

I don't know who to sit with, or who to talk to. I'm a big mess. I grab a seat and eat my lunch with the Six Chicks – the popular girls, the people I've known and hung out with for all of middle school.

Maybe it's time to become the true person I am.

I am, after all, the outcast.

-Brittany Krystantos; the teenager who is NOT your average teen....

Now...

I don't smoke or drink or go to raves anymore-- does that make me "not your average teen"? Instead of going out and partying on weekends, I read books with soulful, healing messages to bring peace and positive inspiration into my life. Last summer I started yoga after what therapists call a "depression"; what I call "being in a state of emptiness". Not too many teens spend their weekends having "slumber parties" with their grandparents, do they? I don't gossip or call other girls "sluts" behind their backs. I've tried to be like everyone else; to become your "average teen". The result is… it never worked.

So, I guess I'm not your average teen. I am fully okay with that term.

The Awakening

5 YEARS AGO

Many kids at age 12 have never been to a funeral. This is my fourth.

I am getting to see what a long life my great-grandparents lived. I got a call from my mom to say that Nana Shirley, who is 92, "just took her last breath".

That was not easy to hear. It was the day of my dance show. My mom was supposed to come and watch me dance on the stage, but she couldn't, because my grandmother was on her deathbed. And then, hearing those words, "Nana Shirley is gone", five minutes before I was needed on stage, was earthshattering.

I am wearing my black clothes. We're at the funeral home. We are all crying. My mom is beside me. My sister is on the other side. My grandmother and my aunts are on the other side of the room. My cousins are in the room, too. The whole family is here to celebrate the life of Nana Shirley.

In this moment, I think: "We all die and are all reborn. People are born every day, every minute, every second, and people die every day, every minute and every second. That is life."

My tears aren't coming anymore as that thought hits me: This is the circle of life. We die and we are reborn.

In this moment I have learned one important thing: to not give up on my dreams, to keep fighting for them, because one day I will end up just like Nana Shirley, under the ground. And my life better mean something.

My eyes are opened. No longer will I be the same person.

I am officially awakened.

TWO YEARS LATER

I still don't have the answers I want. I search. I search and search. But nothing comes to me.

I know, in my heart, there is something more out there in the world. I need answers. Who am I? Everyone tells me: "You're sixteen. You don't need answers now." I disagree. I'm on a mission.

It's 4 a.m. I can't get to sleep. So I get up and walk out to the back yard balcony. I can't stop crying. I can't stop doubting. I never wake up wanting to be alive, because life keeps getting worse and worse. Every day I wake up and have to go to the one place I hate. School. I see people who laugh at me and call me freak.

"Why am I living?" I call to the sky. "I am such a mistake!"

All of a sudden I am aware that my tears have stopped. I look up and see the sky differently. It is clear, with millions of bright stars. My body feels lighter. My hands have stopped shaking.

Then I realize my mother is here beside me.

"Everything okay, Sweetie?" she says.

"Yes, Mom," I tell her. I'm okay now. The empty void is gone. I want to live the greatest and brightest life, like those stars. I want to create dreams. I want them to come true."

My mom hugs me tightly.

"I've been waiting for this day to come," she says, "when you can smile because you're truly happy with life."

It's more than looking up at the stars. At this moment I realize there is no point in living with darkness and negativity. Tonight I see beauty. I see love. I feel stillness. And I know this is my second awakening.

I see people differently now. I see the world differently, too. I don't just see details; I see the bigger picture.

The way I treat others and the way I act is completely different than the person I was before my awakenings.

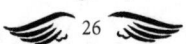

I have been telling people – telling my classmates and my friends, but not many people understand yet. Some can see that I have changed, but they can't put a finger on it. Some people can't see it at all, or they just don't get it, and they're laughing at me.

"Brittany," my best friend tells me, "you are the joke, the talk and gossip of the school. People are calling you weird. They're laughing at you because you told someone you're spiritual. Keep your beliefs to yourself, girl."

Maybe what I saw on that starry night was only meant for me to see. A star doesn't change everyone's lives. Not everyone shares the same awakening.

The Gift

We are all stories. We are all on this earth to start one, continue it, and finish it.

Some people take their last breath without finishing their story.

I walk around just like everyone else, in the halls, in the malls, in the stores. I look like anyone.

But there's always been one thing that makes me different. I feel things. I sense who people are before they tell me themselves. I can feel in my heart what they've been through. Some people say this is a gift of intuition.

I hide this part of my life from everyone because it's my past. I blocked this ability or gift because it wasn't serving me. This is the first time I've shared it publicly.

My dad always told me: "Brittany, there is no shame in hiding this part of your life. It's cool. It's fascinating. People deserve to know, because maybe other people are dealing with it themselves."

This is where you're thinking, "What the heck?" Or: "Wow, cool! Can you see my grandmother for me?"

No I can't. This is an old gift I locked away. I was a "go to" person. I was a messenger.

I got to a point in my life where being the messenger wasn't serving a purpose anymore. It almost became a burden. I didn't come here to help lost souls understand where they went wrong, or help them to realize how they could do better in the next life. Isn't that what angels are for?

My purpose is to help and guide young souls on this earth, and that is what I now live to do.

Do you have any of these gifts?

If a stranger walks by you and you start to understand who they are without them telling you, then consider seeing a Reiki Master or spiritual coach who can help you control these gifts. Isn't that the beauty of Google? Search one thing and tons of links show up. Do whatever you feel in your heart.

We all have gifts, but some people are more intuitive than others. They live with these gifts every day and it can be overwhelming. They're not ordinary people. So whatever you do, never judge them. They need your support, not your criticism.

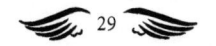

Here are the tools you will be hearing a bunch of times throughout this book, eleven tools that will help you with your life:

TOOL 1: YOUR VOICE MATTERS
Find your belief system. Only listen to that one voice inside your mind, body, and spirit. Don't only listen to the opinions of your teachers, friends, parents or anyone else, because this is your voice, your life, and it matters.

TOOL 2: SEEK POSITIVE FRIENDS
How many times do you actually think about the influence your friends have on you? Never? This is the time to reflect on who is around you. Ask yourself questions. Is my friend positive or negative? Does my friend lift me up or break me?

TOOL 3: FOLLOW YOUR BUTTERFLIES
Ever wanted to do something so badly but you just couldn't seem to do it? When butterflies flew around in your stomach? When sweaty palms or dizziness took over your body? This means your fear and phobia have stopped you. Don't let them.

TOOL 4: FINDING YOUR WORTH
You feel like you suck, that you're worthless. You think nobody will ever love you the way your heart wants. And you tell yourself every day how ugly, fat, stupid and worthless you are. You think about what the world would be like without you in it. This awesome tool is broken down into two great powerful sections: Life and Worth. "Change your life by changing your thoughts, live for something."

TOOL 5: END YOUR ADDICTION AND HABIT
No matter where you go or what you do to distract yourself, eventually reality catches up with you. This is a chance to understand what it is you tend to grasp onto and attach yourself to. Have you ever thought about the habits in your life and the things you can't seem to let go of? Free yourself from negative attachments. Less how do I let it go and more why do I need drugs, food, etc.

I only hope that after all your searching, hard work and discovery, you will be able to say: "This is me and I know exactly who I am."

TOOL 6: FIND YOUR PLACE IN LIFE
What hobbies or activities interest you? What are you most passionate about? Where can you go to feel at peace with yourself? Find your own sanctuary. Think about what you want to be doing in a few years and what excites you.

TOOL 7: WALK THE WALK
How many times have you misjudged, misunderstood or misperceived someone who turned out to be a decent person? "You never truly know someone until you've walked a mile in their shoes." Often we judge people before walking their walk. This is about how can we understand people before doing what most of us do in school: gossip and judge.

TOOL 8: MISTAKES ARE YOUR BIGGEST TEACHER
It's okay to make a mistake. Go ahead and make a mess, make a fuss, make a noise and make the most out of your life. Don't be afraid to fail. Mistakes end up teaching us the most incredible lessons ever.

TOOL 9: BE KIND
In everything you do, be kind to others. When you make someone smile, it's a ripple affect- you will instantly feel happy.

TOOL 10: TRUST YOUR INNER SPARK
Our internal feelings are always right, but our fears get in the way. Find your inner voice and trust it. Keep an open mind.

TOOL 11: LOVE YOURSELF
This is about cultivating positive thoughts about your body, mind and spirit. Letting go of "I hate myself" and learning to say, "I love myself. Damn right."

Have You Ever Felt Like This?

"How could I live my passion when all I have is so much stress to deal with? There's way too much to do; I have school. I have work. I have to make time for my friends. I am totally stressed out! WTF?"

"How can I feel good about myself? Wherever I go, I see someone with a better body, nicer clothes. She has blonde hair and I want hair like hers. He has better grades than I do. She is prettier and gets boys and I am just plain old ugly. If I had any of that, then just maybe I could be happy with myself."

"My life is the worst. My family has no money! Sometimes we don't even have dinner. My friends don't understand what I am going through, they don't know this about me and how can I tell them? I can't just tell them I'm poor and can't even eat dinner with my family! That would be embarrassing."

"I look myself in the mirror and all I see is fat thighs, fat stomach, heavy legs, and big face. And then I see the popular girls at my school, and they are skinny and beautiful. I keep going on diets; I lost five pounds, then I gained it all back. I want to look good, I want boys to look at me but I always seem to be the 'ugly one' in their eyes. I cry myself to sleep every night saying, 'I wish I could look decent enough for somebody to even look at me without wanting to just be friends'."

"My family life is a disaster. They don't stop telling me what to do. My brother expects me to be somebody. My mom expects me to be something and my dad has an entirely different perspective of what he wants me to do in my life. How can I live the life I want, when all these people won't leave me alone to figure out who I am? If only they could stop nagging, stop controlling and stop creating an opinion of me."

"I am not doing well in school, I am a 50 student but my sister is a 90 student. I feel embarrassed. I don't want my parents to think any less of me. I don't want them to think I am the 'stupid child'. My sister is just the smart one in our family. I have other dreams but it doesn't include school. To be honest, I am just bored. I hate sitting in the same seat for two hours, I want to be living life and doing things but I'm forced to sit in a seat for hours a day."

These problems are real, and there's no medicine or cure that can turn these emotions off. I would never ask you to stop feeling the way you do. Are you feeling confused right now? That's okay. Are you feeling lonely right now? That's okay. Are you feeling worthless right now? That's okay.

We have all felt it from time to time. What you're feeling in this moment is similar to the person who sits beside you in math class. The person who walks by you in the hallway of your school, or the person you laugh at, has felt that way too.

Now do you understand why I won't tell you to turn them off? These emotions make all of us one, and if together we could amplify these negative feelings into something positive, then as a generation we can make real changes for ourselves and for others.

I am not a retired teenager. So that means I understand how it feels to be a teenager. I still wake up early (way too early) to go to school. I still sit in boring classrooms, listening to people gossip: "She's fat. She has a big ass. She's stupid. He's a man whore. He uses girls as toys." I felt myself going downhill because of negative emotions. Everything I share with you in this book is because it helped transform my life into not wanting to give up.

CHAPTER ONE
Brave

TOOL 1: Your Voice Matters

8 YEARS AGO

Here I am. Seven years old. Silent. Muted. Not able to speak. I just can't. I keep telling myself tomorrow I will speak. Tomorrow will be the lucky day.

But that day never comes. I don't have it within me to speak. My voice isn't good enough.

I see this cute boy every day I come to class, and I want to sit beside him so badly but I can't. I want to ask him if I can play with him in the park, like the rest of my class.

I just don't have the strength to do that. I sit in the back corner of the room quietly, not speaking to anybody. This is a repeat of the day before. I walk into the class and pick a place to sit in the back corner.

When will the day come where I can actually say, "Teacher, I need to use the restroom"?

I don't know why I can't speak. All I know is my voice is somewhere inside me, but I'm too afraid to let it out. Momma keeps telling me that "my voice is beautiful and others deserve to hear it".

But her words don't give me the courage to speak. I small talk around my family. They're the only people who can hear my voice. A few words to mommy, a few words to daddy, and a few words to Sammy, that's all.

And there's Ryan, the boy I have come to realize is like a brother to me. I've known him for as long as I have been alive. He sits with me in the back corner of my classroom. He speaks for me when I can't, and joins me in my own little world where I hide. Nobody else knows how to reach me or how to get me out of my world.

People keep trying. Teachers talk to me and say: "Hi, Brittany." I can see it in their eyes. They're trying to be 'that person', the one who can get me talk, but it never seems to happen.

People ask me to come play. I really want to join their fun, but I can't find it within me to answer them, so I look to the floor and walk away, silently and quietly. Maybe tomorrow will be the day. Before I go to sleep, I'll pray that tomorrow will be my lucky day, and I will speak to not just Ryan, mommy, daddy and Sammy, but to a teacher, perhaps, or a stranger.

It's my birthday tomorrow, I turn eight, I can feel it. I can sense that tomorrow will be the day that changes my life forever. I can do it.

All it takes is to open my mouth, let the sounds come out of my throat, and use my voice. I can do it.

Eight years later…

I did it. On my eighth birthday I spoke to a teacher, Ms. Pintzov. She had gotten me out of my shell. She helped me embrace the voice I had within me. Never had I shared it with others outside of my world. I told myself, "tomorrow will be the day I speak", and I did exactly that.

I have a voice now. It was a struggle to find the confidence to speak my truth. But I did it. I am different, but so are you, there is not one person in this world who is the same; it is completely impossible. My voice is even softer than an average person's. At least that is what I thought. I wanted to change my voice, and find ways to make it sound deeper. Every time I tried changing my voice there was still a part of myself that felt empty, and as if something was missing. I thought if I changed my voice, then others would like me better.

Maybe this entire time it wasn't others who were the problem - it was me. I needed to accept myself. That includes, accept that my voice is fine just the way it is.

Think about who you are and what you believe in.

We all have the ability to express ourselves; some share their voices through art with singing, dancing, and painting. Others boldly speak out.

Despite what you're feeling, it's important to share what you want in life with others and to believe in yourself, to know you are deserving of what you want.

I don't know about you, but I am so tired of being told what to do and what to think. Have you experienced those annoying teachers in your school- who keep telling you where to go, what to do, how to think or who to be? What about your peers gossiping about your outfit choice: "Such an ugly outfit." They gossip, and spread this rumor that "so and so has the worst outfit choices".

Or how about your friends that keep telling you: "You shouldn't be going to college. University is better." And you are holding tight, before you yell at them to "shut up."

"It's none of your g-d DAMN business," you may be thinking.

Or your parents... Oh this is the most common one. I want to say they do it because they love you, so that's why they like to control your life. But the "why" they do it, isn't important right now. It's the annoyance that bugs us, and makes us rage with anger. And we want to yell once again.

"Sweetie, I think you shouldn't be hanging out with Sasha anymore." "Dear, maybe you shouldn't go out tonight."

And then we get mad, and annoyed, and it seems like we're on our period most of the time. Teenage problems! "Mom, dad, shut the heck up already. Leave me alone. Let me live my own life." I've said this to my parents probably as much as I have yelled at my sister for being a "bitch".

Our thoughts often get influenced and manipulated by the people around us. We have the power to reprogram what we think and how we shall live our lives. How? Living by our morals, and creating our own belief systems. This is my favorite discovery.

Finding your voice requires claiming your power, showing people you can't walk all over me. It's liberating. We all have this ability inside of us to move forward, once we stop resisting our voice, and let it shine for what it truly is.

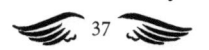

During the first 7 years of my life, I didn't have a voice, which you probably figured from reading the first part of this chapter. I'll just clarify it. Yes, it's true, I didn't speak for seven years. I absolutely understood everything. I saw things that not too many kids would focus on. The doctor said: "put two fingers up. Put five. Put six." And that clarified that I could hear. He said to my parents: "Your daughter is NOT deaf. She hears perfectly fine."

I had chosen not to speak.

I was then called: "the muted daughter." Doctors labeled me with a condition called: **Selective Mutism**, which is a fancy word for, the child only speaks to the people she or he is not comfortable with. Basically, if you're a creep, or scare me, I would NOT talk to you.

It was one of the worst times of my life. So many thoughts consumed me, so many emotions going through me, I couldn't share it with anybody. I didn't want anyone to give me attention for not speaking. I wasn't the spotlight kind of girl. I wouldn't do things to get my parents' attention: "Daddy look at me, I can dance." No. It was the opposite. "Don't look at me. Don't pay attention to me." That's the way I liked it.

I saw many things that were unjust. I lived in frustration with silence.

My dolls were my best friends. I cried to them alone in my room, where I could finally for once let my emotions out. I didn't want anyone to know I was upset. That couldn't happen. I named my favorite dolly: Skye. Because I loved looking up to the sky, it gave me a sense of hope that maybe one day I would talk like most kids. Maybe one day I would have the freedom to be who I never allowed myself to be, the real me.

The one with a voice.

I got tired of feeling invisible. As difficult as it was, there were also benefits. Nobody expected me to speak. Nobody asked me what I wanted to do. I think it became normal. I was known as "the mute girl. The mute daughter. The mute sister. The mute cousin." Nobody expected me to be anything.

Of course I'm a really unpredictable person. I'm definitely full of surprises. At age eight, I finally spoke. I surprised all the teachers, my parents, my family.

I remember being in my kindergarten class and watching the other kids laughing, enjoying their artwork, enjoying their free time, giggling, just "being kids". Then there was me: sitting at the back of the room watching others having fun. I could hear them, loudly giggling, screaming, and whispering to each other.

I always hid in my mom's shadow, and I gave my power away by letting others speak for me. I was voiceless. My mom took the role and became my voice. That was our normal.

The first time I ever spoke, I probably was thinking: "Hey all, I'm here. You better watch out, I'm not going anywhere. Oh and yeah, I'm not planning on belittling myself, and staying in the damn corner for the rest of my life." Okay, maybe I was too young to think that, but that's for sure something I would say now, if I were to go back in time.

*The following is a list of all various stereotypes and opinions associated with each category. I want to know what you believe in. Not what your friends think you should believe in. **This is all about you!!!***

*Maybe have a little fun with this. Circle which stereotype or opinion resonates with you the most. Or underline which opinion you least agree with. This is your chance to rediscover your own beliefs. Become one with your voice. There's only one of you in this world: **one mind, one voice and one you!***

You are…

♡ Nice ♡ Ugly ♡ Rude ♡ Funny ♡ Humorous ♡ Caring ♡ Strong ♡ Smart ♡ Fat ♡ Skinny ♡ Friendly or easy to talk with ♡ Not good enough ♡ Worthless ♡ Amazing

Teenagers are…

♡ Immature ♡ Live in the moment, and don't plan for their future ♡ Wild ♡ Defiant ♡ Only worry about having fun

Family is…

♡ Unconditional love ♡ Stressful ♡ A support system ♡ Annoying

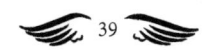

A teacher is…

A role model for my future ♡ Smarter than me ♡ More experienced in life than I am ♡ An educator ♡ Controlling ♡ Mean ♡ Not understanding ♡ A mentor and a leader

Men are…

♡ Strong ♡ Bossy ♡ Better than women ♡ Weak mentally

Women are…

♡ Not paid as much as men do ♡ Weak ♡ Emotional ♡ Caring and Compassionate

Love is…

♡ When two people have a deep emotional, physical and spiritual connection ♡ Only for the weak ♡ Unconditional ♡ Hurtful ♡ Frightening ♡ Vulnerable

Sex is…

♡ Pleasure ♡ Fun ♡ Painful ♡ Only for marriage. ♡ When you bond with someone on a deep level

Working is…

♡ Boring ♡ Challenging ♡ A waste of time ♡ Stressful ♡ Your passion ♡ Enjoyment

Spirituality is…
♡ Religion ♡ Meditation ♡ Singing or chanting Mantras
♡ Living by your own rules

Success is…
♡ Hard to accomplish ♡ For people who are rich ♡ A result of your hard work

Failure is…
♡ Making mistakes ♡ A learning experience ♡ Giving up
♡ Something to learn from ♡ Embarrassing

God is…
♡ Nonexistent ♡ Only for religious people ♡ Male who lives in the clouds
♡ One with love ♡ Light

Religion is…
♡ The teaching of God ♡ Deep ♡ Can be dangerous ♡ Peaceful

A follower is…
♡ Weak ♡ Insecure ♡ Someone who doesn't have their own voice
♡ Someone who needs to be loved and accepted

A leader is…
♡ Caring ♡ Powerful ♡ Inspirational ♡ A role model
♡ Knows more than others ♡ Bossy

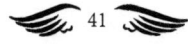

It seems easier than it sounds. All it takes is to "open your lips and a sound should come out", but every time I tried, there was never a noise, never a sound, and my voice never seemed to come out. I remained mute.

Perhaps I am not different than most people. I was mute for seven years, but hasn't there been a time when all of us didn't have a voice? Maybe you were too scared to speak up for what you believe in? Or you were too afraid to be who you are and to speak about what you truly believe in? So you remained mute.

There's always a time in our lives, for all of us when our voice just doesn't come out. You get scared, and so, you put yourself down, by hiding the beautiful voice of yours.

You have a voice. Make sure to not stay silent. Let people hear the sounds you have in you. All it takes is a step of faith. Don't listen to the monsters in your head telling you that "nobody cares about your opinions." That thought right there is my biggest asshole inside of me. When that thought consumes you, tell yourself: "Who cares?" Really though. Who gives a damn about what others think of you?

You have a voice. Let it be heard. You have the power to stop the echoes that continue to play in your mind. Right here, right now, let this be the moment to have your voice be heard, because it matters. All of our voices matter.

Three things you really should pay attention to this month:

1 Don't ever let somebody make choices for you. Been there done that, it sucks.

2 Don't listen to the gossip in your school, whatever opinions they create about you aren't true; what's true is what you believe in.

3 Ever feel hopeless? You see somebody getting laughed at, made fun of at your school and you do nothing. Next time you witness a similar situation, get up do something about it. Stand up for the person. Let your voice help another person.

That's the beauty of your voice.

You were not made to be like everybody else, to think like your friends, to act like your peers or even to listen to other people. Don't follow blindly like sheep waiting to be sheared. *In other words,* don't put yourself in a situation where you're going to be controlled. Take the first step in controlling your own life by believing, thinking and acting upon what you truly feel in your heart.

Your voice can change the world. Yes. It's that powerful.

Let's pledge and promise one thing, together: "We won't stay quiet. We won't stay muted. We will just keep getting louder and louder. Our voice deserves to be heard and to be expressed."

"I am Britt Krystantos and I won't stay quiet. I won't stay muted. I will just keep getting louder and louder. My voice deserves to be heard and to be expressed." Repeat that…. "I am…(your name) and I won't stay quiet. I won't stay muted. I will just keep getting louder and louder. My voice deserves to be heard and to be expressed."

Have you ever felt like nobody is listening to you?
Has there ever been a time where you felt voiceless?

A YEAR AGO

I went to visit my mentor. I call her "Healer T", because she always seems to heal my problems. She kindly said: "When you get home later, please take some time to meditate. And in your mind, talk to the old Brittany: the muted girl. The Britt who had no voice.

Tell her what she never heard as a kid. "Comfort her, mainly nourish her with love. She needs it. Remind Britt that she is not alone. She will be okay."

I walked into my room. I told myself: "Let's go talk to the old me." I lit a candle because I'm dramatic, and needed to make it look spooky. (What can I say? I'm a drama queen sometimes. Don't ask my family. They might say all the time.)

I decided to hold the bracelet I used to wear every day when I was a kid. My name was engraved in it. Whenever I was nervous and scared, my instinctive reaction would be to hold onto this bracelet.

I closed my eyes and let my mind go. I visualized my new self, going back into time. I saw myself entering the old neighborhood I grew up in. I felt my mind going into a meditative state, like a deep dream. Back to when I was silent…

"Brittany, are you there?" I said. "I swear I won't hurt you. If you hear me, then come out of your hiding place. Maybe you're hiding in a corner? Perhaps you're hiding behind a wall where nobody can find you? I think I know exactly where you might be."

I walked into my old townhouse. I opened the door. I saw my mom in the kitchen. I saw my sister dancing and jumping up and down, and my dad talking non-stop about the people in his life. Where was I (old me)?

I walked up the stairs and started saying kindly to myself: "Brittany, I'm coming. You don't need to be scared of me. We are strong. Right now you might be hiding from the world, scared to show people who you are, hiding behind walls, hiding in closets, keeping your mouth shut; but I want to show you and express how it's not bad to speak and share your voice. It's fun to have a voice!"

I walked into my old room. My walls were way too pink, and EW, I had creepy dolls staring right at my bed.

"No sign of Brittany," I said. "Where can she be? I think I know..." I went into my bathroom. She was hiding in her bathtub, and it wasn't filled with water. She had just hidden in the tub because nobody could find her there.

I walked to her. She looked at me. Her eyes were filled with fear. Her beautiful eyes weren't purified, and weren't happy. Anyone who looked into her eyes could see how scared she was to be living her own life with her own voice kept to locked up to herself only.

I took a seat in the bathtub, beside her, putting my hand on her. All her emotions were going through me. I wanted to cry. I wanted to yell. I wanted to take her pain away. But I knew that I needed to be strong for her – for us.

"Brittany," I said. "It doesn't have to be this way. You were given a voice for a reason. Why should we stay quiet when there is a voice waiting to be heard? When there is a voice that can save many people? This voice you hide from the world is the one thing that can change lives.

"Do you know how cool it's been? I spoke on a radio show! I spoke, shared my voice! I did it! No fear. Nothing stopped me. Do you know how uplifting it's been to not be afraid to express what the heck I want to talk about? To wear what I like and to be who I am? It's amazing.

"You are strong. We are strong. We have come this far. You are the old me who never knew your worth. You are the old me who thought about what the world would be without your existence. You thought about how it would feel to take your last breath just so the fear that haunted you could go away."

The old Brittany brought her head up from the ground below us, looking into my eyes, and hugged me. She cried. She cried and cried until the tears couldn't come out anymore.

And she whispered in my ear.

"We have a voice now," she said.

CHAPTER TWO
The Social Struggle

TOOL 2: Seek Positive Friends

FIFTH GRADE.....

I don't have any friends. Me, popular? Yeah, I wish. I have Ryan. My only friend. He spoke for me in kindergarten, when I couldn't. He told the teacher, "Miss? Brittany needs to use the washroom." I was selective about who I spoke to. Ryan felt it was his duty to be my voice.

I'm eleven, and I don't want to have only one friend forever. I want people to look at me, and notice me. Is that too much to ask for? Maybe if I became friends with Tayna? She's popular... she won't accept me, though. I'm way too shy to ever become popular.

I need to start buying new clothes. After school, I'm going to convince my mom to take me shopping. First: get my own pair of UGGS shoes. Second: shop at cool places. Like, American Apparel.

Maybe that will attract popular people into my life. I will finally be seen. Who knows? I can't be a loser forever.

I do exactly that. I get new clothes, I change myself to be just like them... The popular people. I call this "the social struggle", because it's a challenge fitting in.

Am I wearing the right shoes? Am I talking about the right things? Am I just right for this role I'm pretending to be?

I've always wondered: "Where are all the positive friends when everybody is fake?"

15, awakened ~ becoming my truest self, with the a decision to make: should I drift away from my friends or force myself to stay where I am?

THREE YEARS AGO...

"Brittany, you're so weird. What do you do on the weekend? You never come out with us anymore."

My friends don't get me. They'd rather laugh at me, make fun of me, pinpoint my flaws. Why am I sitting with them? I'm hurting myself by hanging out with the people who make fun of me. They give me a headache, literally. They give me anxiety. They make my hands sweat. They make my stomach flutter with fear. I wish I could walk away from them. I wish I had the confidence to leave them.

I'm scared to be a loner though. I'm scared to not have anyone to sit with during lunch.

I'm sitting beside the popular girls. We call each other *"The Six Chicks"*. We just formed a circle in the atrium of our school. I'm laughing, and making fake smiles, pretending like whatever they just said was funny. In reality... it *so* wasn't.

SIX CHICKS,

That was us, the group that brought all of my insecurities out,

The group that made me feel self- conscious about myself,

The group I never showed my true self too,

The fear of them not liking me scared me too much,

Thinking popularity was the way to achieve life,

This group; it made me question everything,

Who were we?

*There was chick #1 "**The Shopper**":*
She always kept up with the latest trend,

*There was chick #2 "**The Gossiper**":*
She judged everyone, everybody, everything,
You wouldn't tell her your darkest secrets,
She gossiped. Looking at ones flaw.

*There was chick #3 "**The Chiller**":*
She was always chilling, Very relaxed,
Always staying out of drama and out of your way. She was just there. People naturally gravitated towards her because she would never judge.

*There was chick #4 "**Life of the Partier**":*
She always got invited to the best parties,
She had boys running after her,
She never said no to a great party.

*There was chick #5 "**The Faker**":*
She always seemed to be happy,
We would all question: "is she really this happy? Or is she faking it?"
She would pretend to love everyone.

*There was chick #6 "**The Outcast**":*
This was ME. *The outcast.*
I tried hard to be like them. I tried to be average and to fit in. I tried shopping. I tried partying. I tried HU (hooking up) [making out] with two boys at one party. I tried venting and talking about my latest crush. It all didn't work. It made me less cool. I always seemed to fail.

These girls were my six chicks. People I once knew. They were my entire life when I was 14. They were my clique. We walked together. We stayed together. We ate together. We did each others make up and hair.

They were the life of a lie I once lived.

I'm not making fun of what they do, because the truth is most of you might do the exact thing. It's what we do to try to survive the social struggle. I get it.

You can say the last chill I ever went to was a chill with the 'six chicks', which ended badly. I went to the washroom, and afterwards as I was walking down the stairs into the basement where my friends were, I overheard some of them talking about me.

"Brittany is so weird," someone said. "The things she says are stupid. This girl is crazy. I don't like hanging out with her. Why did you invite her? She just keeps getting weirder and weirder by the day." Though, I did hear, "The Shopper girl" did stick up for me. I give her credits.

Tears welled up in my eyes. I tried to stay strong. "Brittany, prove them wrong, you're strong and they can't defeat you," I told myself. I held my tears in. I didn't want them to see me cry because that makes them win automatically. I went into the room, gathered all the strength inside of me and said, "Hey guys, I'm not feeling good, leaving now, thanks for inviting me, bye."

How do you find great friends in high school? How do you find trustworthy friends when your main concern is having the most friends and being the "cool girl or the popular boy"?

I always had more likes on my Facebook profile pictures than most of my friends in grade nine, my first year of high school. I was always one of the first to be invited to the 'cool' parties. I thought that going to 'those' types of parties made me accepted, but I was wrong. The expectation to be 'cool' was to drink your brains out and smoke until your lungs hurt. Growing up is difficult. Most of us just want to fit in and have our peers accept us. We sometimes create an image of who we are, and do things out of character just to belong.

Are you the girl who "slept with four boys at the biggest party of the year", or are you the boy who "banged the most girls in a week"? Are you really the person who wanted to do that? Or did you do it for acceptance and popularity purposes? Are you someone who never felt accepted by your peers for having boundaries/ morals? Do you take every opportunity that comes your way to impress others, just to be 'cool'? Are you someone who would live up to those types of standards just to fit in?

If so, then congrats, you're a teenager, just like myself.

January 24, 2012
My last party

Dear diary,

I didn't want to go to the party. My friends forced me to go.

Why do I listen to others all the time? Why do people always have control over me? I think tonight's experience has given me the strength to stick up for myself and say no whenever I want to.

I wanted to hang out and chill at home. But no. They said: "Don't be a loser. Let's go party!"

I really didn't want to go.

It was a house party. The six of us walked there. I was annoyed and in a bad mood. This wasn't what I had in mind for my Friday night

We walked into the house and all I heard was out-of-control screaming and partying. I just wanted to escape. I thought: I want to leave and go home. I counted the clock all night. I kept reminding myself: if I leave now, they'll never talk to me again. My friends will think I'm a loser and a weirdo.

My friends left me to take shots and get wasted. So I stood alone in one of the rooms. People laughed and were wasted. Some boys checked me out. And all I could think was: "This is SO not me!"

When we finally left, I knew this would be my last high school party. I was only in grade 9, but I just knew all the pretending wasn't worth it. Partying wasn't my scene. I don't drink. I don't smoke. So if I'm not accepted as ME — as an average person — it's their loss.

And if they classify me as "weird", and "not your average teen", then so be it

After I followed the popular kids for almost three years, there was so much I learned. I did everything they asked me to do, not because I wanted to, but because the thought of losing my spot at the "popular" table frightened me. The thought of being alone without friends haunted me. I was like a lost dog who would follow any stranger who had a treat. My "treat" was popularity. I did whatever it took to be part of the group.

I was the outcast all along, not knowing if I should follow the leader or leave them forever. Until my grade nine party, I realized that if I was too scared to say "I don't feel like going to a party tonight" to my friends, they weren't my true friends.

If you are holding back anything that makes you unique from your friends, consider changing your friends. If anyone has power over you to make you feel like you have to change, especially your morals, they're not friends. Don't choose friends just so you won't end up being alone and feeling like a "loser" or because you want to be accepted. Choose them because you love their energy and how they make you feel when they're around you.

When I developed my physical voice at age seven, I saw friend groups that were already formed. At recess, I noticed that everyone seemed to know where they belonged and who their friends were.

But then there was me: the girl who was friendless and alone. I thought: "What step should I take next?" I looked over at some cool kids sitting in a circle. I wondered what it would be like to be them, to be a cool kid. I kept asking myself: "What would it be like to feel like I am a somebody, and that I matter?"

All I ever wanted was to feel average.

When I was around my friends at school, I put on an act: a big smile, pretending I was perfect.

Once I got home, I felt alone, like something was missing. Perhaps it was because I couldn't call my so-called friends when I had a real problem. I couldn't tell them about what I was going through or what I believed in. I found my voice at age seven, but I lost it again. I became silent in another way. My voice was hiding my true and real self behind some sort of wall that I put up when my friends were nearby.

I realized soon after I started high school, in grade nine (Miner Niners, the seniors called us), things began to bother me. It stung when my friends laughed at me. It took time to deal with it, though. I didn't just one day wake up and completely stop talking to these people. It took time to drift away from them.

I didn't find it amusing to make fun of other people or to gossip about them behind their backs. This wasn't a world I wanted to be part of anymore.

The scariest part was that I didn't know if I could find a friend who would lift me up when there was no one to talk to. I had to decide: "Who will I eat lunch with? Who will stick with me?"

Nobody wants to be known as the odd one out. The hardest thing was knowing people were looking at me and thinking I wasn't cool anymore. I was no longer popular.

It was either: be fake or be myself.

I had to pick which one was more important.

I have received comments on my blog from teens who ask me questions about finding the "right" friends.

"Brittany, what do I do? My friends laugh at me. I am the joke of the group, and they never take me seriously. How am I supposed to just walk away from them when I've known them for most of my life?"

"My friends make me drink when I don't want to. My friends say if I don't smoke, I will be a baby and a loser. How did I end up getting myself stuck in this situation? Never did I think I would become this person!"

"My friends laugh at me because they say I don't wear nice outfits. They say I need to care more about my appearance. It's true. I don't care to dress up to look perfect, because nobody is perfect, and I don't want to be a fake. I think it's time to leave them behind. Thanks for helping me realize that."

"Actually, I have a really great support group. I am a misfit and an outcast, and I only have one friend. But I am happy with myself. I don't need popularity to define me or to make me feel happier, because I'm happy with myself."

Some of us are lucky and have great friends. Others aren't so lucky, because they have bad ones – the ones who laugh at them. The ones who make them cry. The ones who question their existence.

If this sounds anything like you, circle the statements in the checklist that relate most to you. Have fun with this. You could underline the statements that don't resonate with you and highlight the ones that do. Make the most out of this.
You're one step closer to finding yourself.

Friend Checklist

♡ My friends don't support me

♡ My friends are all so judgmental that they laugh at me and call me names

♡ I can't share my dreams or secrets with them

♡ I can't let my friends really know me

♡ I don't know how to keep friends for very long

♡ I don't know how to tell my friends "No"

♡ I don't like having friends

Don't you want people to love you for you and not for the person you pretend to be? Friends, good or bad, have the ability to influence how you think and act. But it is up to you to say "NO" and to listen to your voice.

Everyone has the ability to have power or control over us. Bad friends can actually determine the person you never thought you would become. But when you choose good friends, they can help you become a better person. Their energy lights us up, isn't it cool how that works?

There's a saying:

"Why walk in the fire alone?"

If we could walk in the deepest fire with someone we could lean on, and if that person could make us feel as though everything will be fine, why can't we make it our mission to find such a person?
Friends can build you up or pull you down. My friends tore my heart into little pieces, and one day it shattered in my face – at that awful party.

Have you ever felt like your surroundings bring you in a bad mood?

SURROUND YOURSELF WITH THE RIGHT PEOPLE

I finally decided my group, "The Six Chicks", weren't the people who could build and lift me up.

Slowly but surely, I did it. I walked away from them.

I walked into the fire alone, not knowing who would be there for me. Who would make me smile? Laugh? Feel like I'm whole again?

Once I started to walk, I found others who made me feel as though I matter. And when I walked out of that fire, my true friends were waiting to take my hand.

In the space below, write the name of your friend. Tell me some of your friend's positive qualities. If you can't think of any, that's okay, because it might give you the answers you've needed for a long time. If you don't feel like writing in this book, get a journal or a piece of paper, or make a note on your phone.
Maybe it's time to switch your friends around. Tell me about them!

My friend

My friend

My friend

When you choose to surround yourself with positive friends, you'll notice how happy and alive you'll begin to feel. You'll realize you don't have to be anybody you don't want to be. All you have to be is yourself. Wear baggy clothes; wear your hair up; wear whatever your heart wants. Be **you**.

If you continue to hang around with negative people, you'll notice they'll pull you down. They'll give you a hard time for not doing what they want you to do. They'll point out your flaws in front of people. They'll hurt you. Walk away from them.

And if you're anything like me, they'll make you drain, and give you the worst headaches. No joke, it's true, it happened.

Friends create the environment in which you can grow and blossom into the person you really are or shrink into a jock/cheerleader cliché.

Nobody wants to be the odd one, but wouldn't you rather look back at your high school experience knowing you were real? Or would you rather remember being a big fake?

Three years have gone by. I'm walking into the hallway of my school. The bell just went for Math. BORing. My old friend (I'll call her "Abby") just walked pass me. She didn't say a thing. Not: "Hey, Britt, how are you?" or: "Hey, Britt, I've missed you!" – nothing. She just looked at me. She was like a ghost. A stranger. She was not like someone I used to spend whole weekends with.

Do I feel empty? Do I feel lost without her friendship? No. I feel stronger knowing that the right people, the people who love me and lift me up, surround me.

Someone once said to me: "Stand up on this chair and try to pull me up to stand on it with you."

I said: "That's a little hard, don't you think?"

"Exactly," was the answer. "It's easier to pull someone down than lift someone up."

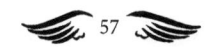

Fourth grade...

"Teacher, I don't like Meital. She's always copying my work," I lied (Actually, I copied hers). "She's annoying. Why do you always put her in my group? Don't you understand? We don't like each other! Are you trying to make me mad? Because I am very mad right now!"

"Brittany," my teacher answered. "You don't like her. She has no problem with you. In life, you're going to come across people you don't like. One day you'll notice she's not so bad."

And now...

I want to make a special thank you to someone: to Meital. This girl found me crying one day. And she became "my everything" – my sister, my friend and my family, all in one. She was the one person who showed me that it's okay to be an "outcast" and it's actually fun being a "loser".

If being yourself makes you both an "outcast" and "loser", so what?

Every lunchtime, Meital sat with me in a hallway where no popular people would dream of hanging out. She stayed with me during the most terrible nightmare in my life. What kind of friend eats lunch with you in a staircase rather than being comfortable sitting at a table in the cafeteria?

If you have a friend who has been "your everything" during the nightmare of your life, make sure you say "thank you".

Meital walked into the fire with me. Thank you, Meital. I love you.

Don't waste your time with people who will never appreciate and value everything you have to offer.

Try this affirmation: "I choose to surround myself with people who make me smile.

Three years ago....

It was just a normal weekend with my friends. We called ourselves "The Six Chicks". Six of us headed downtown to the huge Toronto exhibition park called the CNE.

All of us thought we were so cool because we went on the subway without any parents. "How cool is this?" I asked myself. "I'm with my friends!" But then I thought: "Why do I have to keep thinking about what I say to them? Why do I feel so nervous?"

Maybe this feeling of nervousness had charged through me because I couldn't say the words that were in my mind. I couldn't be myself.

I became increasingly aware that I couldn't be who I was with these people. I didn't even know who I was. I realized my "friends" were laughing at me and making me feel like some kind of joke. I wasn't comfortable around them. But I didn't want to lose them, either, because I didn't want to be a loner. So I put all my doubts out of my mind and decided they were awesome, great, and that they accepted me.

We went to a psychic station at the fair. I thought it would be fun to get my palm read. It was only $10, so I figured it was probably fake, but worth the try. I told my friends what I wanted to do. "Are you crazy?" they said, as if I was. I didn't know what to say. I didn't know the "right" or "cool" response to something like that.

I went to the psychic booth anyway and held out my palm to the woman. Amazingly, everything she told me came true. How could a $10 reading be so correct?

She said: "Your friends aren't true ones. They don't understand you. They talk behind your back. I think deep down you know this is true, but you're too afraid to admit it."

She was right. I thought if I lost them, I'd be a wreck. I couldn't imagine being in high school without any friends.

"Don't worry," the psychic added. "In about four months there will be a big fight that separates all of you."

Four months after my visit to the psychic, a big fight blew up among my friends, and "The Six Chicks" were no longer.

It was a big break. The six of us used to eat lunch together every day. We hung out on the weekends. We had fancy slumber parties. We traded clothes and shared everything we bought with each other. We told each other about our newest crush and talked until midnight. We complained about our parents. We did each other's hair and makeup. We practiced looking sexy (and looked pretty silly as a result). We were close. We were like family, at least that is what I pretended. And then we were strangers.

Writing got me out of my funk.

It became a place where I could express myself, and acknowledge my true feelings. I want to give you that same opportunity. My mentor told me: "Take out a pen, get yourself a journey. And write how you feel." I'm telling you that too, write how your day was, write about how you're feeling (negative or positive). Maybe, write about how annoying your peers were at school or simply talk about how amazing your day has been. Did someone call you names? Did your parents piss you off? Let this be a time for you to start writing your own story. It starts with your thoughts, which ends up becoming your life story. On every chapter there will be a place for you can write, take it or leave it, option is up to you.

CHAPTER THREE
Be Fearless

Tool 3: Follow Your Butterflies

> Expose yourself to your deepest fear; after that, fear has no power, and the fear of freedom shrinks and vanishes. You are free.
>
> – JIM MORRISON

Sometimes we just need to tell ourselves: "Just fuck it" – and let it get us past our greatest fear. When I get scared or anxious (which happens a lot), that's my mantra:

Just fuck it.

My mentor Kimberly told me: "So fucking what? Go and follow those butterflies, and when you get scared repeat those exact words: *"So fucking what?"*

It is important to understand why we fear, before we go chasing butterflies.

We all want to be loved. Right? *Daddy love me. Mommy look at how great of a dancer I am.* We all want to be accepted. *Like buying trendy clothes to fit in.* We want to be wanted and to be good enough. But sometimes along our journey there are things we just can't cross. This is called fear. Why though? We live in a really messed up world.

It's poisoned with our fear, controlling us into not doing something.

Imagine a three year old running around the house. She's throwing things. She's laughing and yelling. She wants to watch The Wiggles or Elmo. She lives in the moment.

She's doing what kids do. They don't even think about the future unless it's what toy to play with next. She doesn't think about what's right or wrong.

In her unleashed enthusiasm, the three-year-old picks up her daddy's business file and throws it, papers flying, across the room.
Her daddy is under stress from work, she can't possibly understand, he loses it on her. He yells at her. And spanks her.

She cries as if the world has come to an end. But she's not crying because of the sting of the spanking. She's crying because it shocked her and hurt her feelings. "My daddy doesn't love me," she thinks.

It's one of many emotional wounds she will face in life, but now it gets tied up with a feeling she hasn't had before: fear – fear that he will spank her again.

Her mind is now programmed to thinking: daddy doesn't love me. She will always think every man that comes into her life, will not be good enough, because her mind will always tell her: No man will love me, because daddy doesn't.

In her own three-year-old way, she begins to build a wall.

14 YEARS LATER: 17 YEARS OLD

She says no to every boy who wants to take her out for coffee. She pushes away friends. She doesn't want to take the chance that they'll hurt her.

So that's what I mean about a messed up world. We all have emotional pain and misery that we need to heal.

Most people, if they're lucky, start out as free and joyful children. But so often our messed up world teaches them "I suck" and "I'm not good enough".

We all hurt deeply. Let's see if we can release this fear.

Follow your butterflies

Face your fear head on. As you do one thing you're afraid of, turn it into a chance to release something rather than turn it into your addiction. Sometimes we do one thing we're scared of repeatedly because there's a kind of hype to it. But fear is an illusion.

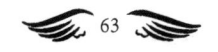

Your tummy might hurt. Your mouth might get dry. You might feel dizzy. Whatever tingling feelings travel through your hands, know that it's just your butterflies. Always chase them. When we learn to face our fears, we become unstoppable. "Ride these emotions", is what my mentors had told me before.

You're probably wondering: Why is this crazy girl telling me to follow my butterflies? I don't mean real ones. I mean the ones you feel in your stomach, the ones that come to you while you're feeling anxious. It's the only way to keep your emotional wounds from stopping you. That's how you become unstoppable.

We all have a choice. We can live in fear, or we can become fearless. Which will you decide? I challenge you to chase one fear per week and hope that it will show you that fear is an illusion. You'll see what a difference it will make and how good you'll feel afterwards.

Imagine a lifetime of being fearless and unstoppable!

Your Butterflies/Fear Checklist

Please circle, highlight or make a note of the statement or question that resonates with you the most. Be honest.

- ♡ I am afraid of animals
- ♡ Snakes scare the crap out of me
- ♡ Leaving my home frightens me
- ♡ What if I don't ever find true love and live alone forever?
- ♡ Walking into the hallways of my school scares me
- ♡ I'm afraid others will judge me
- ♡ I'm scared of death
- ♡ I'm afraid of failing a test
- ♡ I'm afraid I won't ever be good enough
- ♡ Being in a large crowd makes me anxious
- ♡ I'm afraid to not be enough for my parents
- ♡ The future scares the crap out of me
- ♡ I'm afraid to walk in the dark

Are you afraid of heights? Can't touch a cat without freaking out? Can't speak in front of a crowd?

Something must have happened to make you feel that way. Were you ever on a tall building when somebody said something mean to you? Did you ever, as a kid, touch a cat and it bit you?

I used to dislike speaking in front of the class. Before my teachers could choose me to answer a question, I'd give them a death glare that said: DON'T YOU DARE PICK ME! My mouth would go dry. My palms got sweaty. My stomach turned and twisted and made noises.

I had two options. I could have chased that butterfly or run away. Why was I so nervous, anyway? Nobody even paid attention. Most of my peers were too busy taking selfies, or tweeting and texting. Not once did they look up.

But what I discovered was that my fear wasn't just a feeling or an emotion. It went deeper than that. I thought about this a lot. Why did I dislike speaking in front of a crowd?

Bingo. I discovered the answer. I thought I wasn't good enough. "My voice is pointless," I told myself. "It doesn't deserve to be heard. I'm worthless."

So I carried these thoughts throughout my life. And every time I had the chance to speak, I'd get nervous. I came from not having a voice to having one. What a crazy time!

The reason I became anxious before I spoke in front of the class was because I had emotional wounds that I wasn't aware of. I was poisoned with the infection of fear.

People who fear the unknown or unusual can't take a new road. It scares the heck out of them. They tend to never try new things, go to new places, hang out with a different crowd. Any kind of mystery or "unknown" causes them anxiety.

But they are the very people who need to be challenged to do something out of the ordinary. Are you such a person?

Have you ever had a crush on someone but you had no idea what to say to him or her? Your stomach would hurt; your hands would shake; your palms would be wet; your mouth would be dry. That's fear.

I was at an event one time. There was music playing. I looked over towards the DJ booth, and saw a really – and I mean really – hot guy. I watched him as he pressed buttons and chose tunes that got the crowd moving. He looked like a hot bad boy.

I got butterflies in my stomach. When we find a really attractive person, we want to speak to him or her, but we don't know how to. Those butterflies keep trying to convince us to run away. Our speech stops and we're silent.

My mom noticed me staring at him.

"If you don't go over there and speak to him now, you will regret it," she said.

I kept hearing the voice of my mentor. "If you're ever nervous or you fear something," she told me, "that feeling in your stomach is a sign that you should do it. Always do what makes you want to escape."

Always follow the butterflies, I said to myself. It was *now* or *never*.

I walked up to the DJ booth. I spoke too fast and tried to introduce myself. I tried not to sound as scared as I was. My stomach was killing me and my hands were shaking. I blabbed away at him about how I loved music and I don't know what else I said.

It wasn't the result that made me happy. It was the fact that my butterflies gave me a chance to overcome a fear. Afterwards, I walked into the bathroom and literally did a happy dance. I must have looked like a fool, shaking my hips, flipping my hair back and forth and singing: "Yay! I did it!"

After that event, I became unstoppable and fearless.

Short. Sweet. Simple.

1 Understand what you're most frightened of.

2 Listen to your fear carefully. Become mindful of the way it affects your emotions, your body.

3 Whatever your fear is, go after it. This is the time when you need to experience accomplishment. Overcoming something brings happiness. Even if it only lasts for a few seconds, at least you will see how it feels.

4 Be proud of yourself. Smile, dance, jump, go into a washroom and flip your hair like I did. People might think you're a little crazy, but who cares?

People don't know this about me because it's not something I'm open about sharing. I mean, I wouldn't feel comfortable sharing it on Facebook. But I think I should share it with you.

I have trust issues. You're probably thinking: "Don't we all?" Well, yeah. You're right. We all have trust issues because we've all been hurt.

I thought I didn't trust others. But what I discovered is that I don't trust myself. It's not as if I haven't tried. Every morning I wake up and say: "I trust myself". But this affirmation isn't working.

Why would it work, when I didn't take any action? I said "No, sorry…" to every boy who asked me out. I wouldn't give him a chance. I'd delete his number and ignore his text messages.

One day I was really upset. I thought about how I disconnected myself from people. And then I called one of my mentors, Emily.

I said: "Here's the issue. I can't seem to trust others."

"I think," she said, "you can't trust yourself."

"I'm scared I'll get hurt," I said. I'm scared I won't be good enough for him. I don't trust myself enough to make a relationship work, because I do dumb things. I'm nothing special, so why should I deserve to have a relationship?"

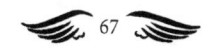

I continued: "I do want to change my habits, though. I want to stop being afraid of opening myself up."

"Wait a minute," she said. "See how your trust issue comes from thinking you're not good enough? You are better than enough, and any guy would be lucky to be with you. I think we should make an action plan."

Oh, gosh, I thought. What next?

"Next time a guy asks you out," she said, "I want you to go out with him. You have the power to say yes or no. If you don't feel anything more than a great friendship, that's your choice. Don't let your emotional wounds scare you away from a potential friendship or an amazing relationship."

So I did exactly that. I said "Yes" to the next guy who asked me out for coffee, and we developed a wonderful friendship.

When I'm talking to an intimidating person, I like to pretend I'm speaking to the toddler version of them. If you're scared of a big man with muscles, and he looks like he might be able to beat you in a fight, then just imagine him as a kid, running around asking: Momma, I want more cake.

My mentor told me: "always imagine them as a small kid wandering around the playground." I tried it. And damn it's funny. Seriously though. If you're talking to a bitchy woman, and she's scaring the crap out of you, look her in the eye, and see her transforming into a little girl. Try not to laugh, because you don't need her calling you names, or lashing out.

Goal of the day: Let's not allow our pain to stop us from doing things that are unknown. If there is ever a chance to do something interesting, say YES without knowing the outcome. Let's promise not to live our fear but to get rid of it. If you're ever scared, just try my mantra:

Just fuck it. Or so fucking what?

Tell me about your fears. Or vent about your day. What scares you the most?

CHAPTER FOUR
Life

Tool 4: Finding Your Worth

October 4, 2014

I hate myself
I wish my pain could end
I am worthless
There is no point in living anymore
Nobody will love me
I'll never be an accomplishment
Raging thoughts: "What would the world be without me"?

I was so in the dark. Where was my worth? My chest felt heavy. Waking up every morning became a drag. How could I possibly enjoy life?

There was only one time when I actually dreamed of what the world would be like without me.

Two years ago

Nobody loves me. My parents don't understand me. I don't even understand myself. When I look at myself in the mirror, all I see is a stranger.

I'm dumb. I must be. I never get good marks in school. I'm ugly. I must be. No boys pay attention to me.

My parents keep yelling at me to go out. "Go to Tanya's house," they say. "Just get out for awhile."

What if I don't want to go out? What if I don't feel welcome at Tanya's house?

I hate myself so much. Sometimes I look at the bathtub and wonder: "What would the world be without me?" I mean, I don't really plan on ending my life. I still have to prove myself to some people. But still, I think: If I slipped under the water in the tub, everything would end. But not yet. I need to live for something. I need to find hope. I need to discover ways of being happy. I have people I want to inspire. I have things I want to do. I have a mission to change the world.

I can't do that if I'm not here.

READY TO FIND YOUR WORTH?

Life can be beautiful. If I had ended my life, I would have missed the smiles I've put on people's faces. I would have missed the chance to look at myself in the mirror and finally say: "I found life! I'm alive and I love every second of it!"

If you think your life doesn't matter and if you are now living the way I once was, this is for you. I understand how it feels: being lonely and sad, and feeling unwanted. It's the worst feeling.

Beat that feeling, get rid of it, you're alive, you're fucking alive, do you realize that?

Life comes at us from all corners. It wears us down. It demolishes us piece by piece before we find the light and become whole. People think it's simple, easing the pain by ending your life. But it's not simple at all. What good comes out of ending your road and letting others defeat you?

Our heart grows, gets stronger, becomes clearer. We care about finding the light, but we fail to find it time after time. Eventually we believe there is no light and there is no miracle.

"If it doesn't exist," we tell ourselves, "Why should I keep searching for it?"

If you look a little closer, breathe a little deeper, you can believe a little more that a fire will blaze in your heart.

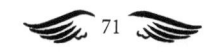

The world still needs your beautiful presence.

Never forget that. You may have heard of someone who committed suicide. Maybe you've heard about it through social media. Maybe you have read about it on the news. Maybe you know someone who tried it but didn't do it and got help. We all hear about it. It happens.

If there is a day when you can't move, when you just can't seem to get out of your bed – when you have no desire to do anything, please hear my voice: "You can do it!" Let those words give you a flicker of hope so you can get up and have strength for the day.

What does strength mean? Where does it come from? If there is strength, there must be weakness. You are not perfect and either am I. No one in this world is perfect because it's impossible to be perfect.

If you get to the point when you feel as if you're at the end of your road, please talk to somebody. Talk to your parents. Speak to your favorite teacher. Talk to your guidance counselor, or at least talk to someone you trust.

If you're having thoughts about ending your life, remember what and who you will be leaving behind. Suicide is never the answer. It solves nothing. It might end your hurt, but it creates a world of pain for those who love you.

Picture your mother walking into your room to wake you up for school and you're lying there in a pool of your own blood. Do you really think nobody will care or be affected? You're wrong, because everyone will be affected. Your parents will have one fewer kid. Your siblings won't have you in their lives anymore. Your grandparents will have one less grandchild. Your cousins won't have their best friend. Your best friend won't have his or her other half. How are they going to move on and be okay without you in their lives?

The teachers who knew you will feel regretful and ashamed of themselves for not being there for you. You think no one loves you, but you're wrong, because the day of your funeral, tons of people from your school, your family, your friends and your community, dressed in black, will gather. They'll have tears running down their faces and they'll be wondering what they could have done differently to save you.

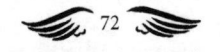

For the rest of their lives, your parents will blame themselves for your death. They will constantly wonder what they should have done differently.
Giving up won't fix anything. The only thing it will do is to end the pain that haunted you. You were given the gift of life – to meet new people, to change the world in some way, to love with passion, to experience new adventures. Just understand this:

LIFE wants you to keep riding the challenges.

Nothing is ever so bad that you have to kill yourself over it. There's always a way to get back up from a mountain you think you can't climb or a weight you think you can't carry.

I need you in this world, and without you things aren't the same. Without you, this generation isn't completed. We need you to stay and climb mountains with us. So stay. Stay with us. Stay for me.

Life is asking you to continue to fight past times when you feel like giving up. Let your strength make it through the rocky bumps.

This is your life. Right now, and right in this moment. Fight for it. And never forget: ***I see you***

Does life ever get too hard? When life gets to overwhelming, I stop everything I'm doing and I ask myself this: "how do I feel?"
Tell me how YOU feel.

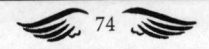

CHAPTER FIVE
Worth

TOOL 4: Finding Your Worth
(continued)

Ready to understand that knowing your worth is far greater then everything else?

Dear Diary,

I don't know what to say. I was told thoughts become things, and if "we can guide our thinking, our lives will change."

But is that true?

I can't stop crying. Can't stop thinking I'm not good enough. Can't stop thinking I'm worthless.

I can't get these thoughts out of my mind. "You're so ugly, Brittany! You'll never be anything! You're so dumb!"

Life just sucks.

I don't believe the women who told me: "Find your worth, because once you understand how worthy you are, your life will be transformed."

Such BS.

Every time I look at myself in the mirror, I see my eyes, my blonde hair, my legs, my body, my everything. And all I see is ugly. Worthless. Not good enough.

If that's all I feel, how is it possible to find my worth?

Sincerely,

Annoyed Britt

I didn't feel good enough. But I tried. I just didn't know how.

I heard: "Change your thoughts and your life changes for the better". But it isn't that easy. It's changing something you're used to. We become attached to our habits. The word "change" can be a scary thing.

I walk down the streets and I see people so unhappy with themselves. I see crying. Fighting. Hatred. I see people living in insecurity. I rarely see people living in confidence.

What a messed up world we live in.

We all think we're not good enough. We say: "I'll fail my exam. I'll get fired from my job. People won't like my book. I won't be good enough for him. He's going to dump me. She won't want to be my friend."

This negative thinking ruins us. It drains us and creates misery.

Think about all the energy you waste on negative thoughts. What if you spend your energy on positive things? Imagine how differently you'd feel, and how different your life would be.

Maybe you *won't* get fired from your job. Maybe you *won't* fail your exam. Maybe people *will* like your book. Maybe friends *will* stay in your life. And maybe your dream *will* come true.

How *awesome* does that sound?

You can create your own life. If you are a little more confident, your boss will see that and keep you around. If you're a little more confident, you'll know we all make mistakes, and it's okay.

One of my mentors told me: "What you give is what you get back."

Have you ever heard this? What you think is what you get, too – good or bad.

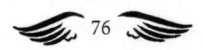

I used to tell people: "control your thoughts". But that's extremely hard, if not impossible. If you're anything like me, you have a million thoughts going on in your mind. What should I wear today? What should I say to him? What to do? Pink or blue? Thought after thought.

So instead of trying to control your thoughts, maybe it's better to *guide* them. When you start to hear that little voice in your head that says: "I suck; I'm ugly" or whatever, become mindful of this dangerous thinking. Instantly replace those thoughts with "I'm beautiful. I'm fantastic."

My mentor told me: "Everyone is responsible for every experience in their lives, even the best and the worst." If you learn to guide your negative thinking into positive thoughts, your life will change.

I think of thoughts like a carousel. They move and never seem to stop. No matter where you are in this time of your life, you will always be thinking about something.

Can we change negative thinking and replace it with positive thoughts? Yes. Let's say you can't even look at yourself in the mirror because you feel horrible about yourself. You hate your eye colour. You hate your legs. You want to be skinnier. You want to be muscular. You want to look like Nick Jonas or have Taylor Swift's body.

If you can't say: "I love myself", pick three things you do like about yourself. Maybe you have nice blue eyes. Maybe you have a caring heart. Maybe you have a good sense of humor. Maybe you have great hair.

Make the time – today – to write in a journal or notebook and come up with three things you like about yourself.

Words can become traps that cause a continuous cycle of negative thinking. Your thoughts don't just stay thoughts. They become your mood, your personality. And they will become your experiences.

We're all tempted to speak negatively at times, but we don't have to give into that temptation. As you think one negative thought, become mindful of it and change it right away.

There are two important words to be aware of: consciousness and sub-consciousness. Or maybe there are simpler words to say the same thing. How about "inner" and "ego"?

Sub-consciousness or "inner" are the thoughts inside our minds that accept us for who we are and direct us to the right path. If you don't like a person, your subconscious will tell you: "This is not my kind of friend."

Should you listen or not listen? It's your choice.

Consciousness or "ego" can be like the bullies we see at school. Instead it's the bullies inside our minds. They can stop us from being who we truly want to be. They can get in our way and instill negative thoughts in our minds. Conscious, or "ego" thoughts might bring on negativity.

I think it's okay to let pain be felt. It's okay to hold onto it for a minute. Cry it out. Feel it. Often we hide our pain behind a smile – behind an act. Surely that isn't the right way to live. It's worse when pain takes over your life, your decisions, and your light.

If you're a person who, in public, seems like the happiest person on earth, but then, alone in your room, you're miserable, you have not paid attention to your feelings.

Take one big breath of negative emotions and then exhale them all out. Do that as often as you need to. They'll no longer control you.

Inhale~ positive energy, positive thinking.

Exhale~ negative energy, negative thinking.

Mirrors

Do you remember when mirrors used to be your best friend? When you were a little kid, did you look at yourself in mirrors with acceptance and happiness?

But if you hate mirrors now and all you see are the thoughts you've been thinking – "I'm ugly", for instance, or "I'm fat", it's time to do something about it.

I asked someone who didn't like what she saw in her mirror, so she cut back a meal a day. Then two meals. Then all of them. I asked her about it.

"Weren't you hungry?" I said.

"It didn't matter how hungry I was," she answered. "I just couldn't eat. The thought that food would turn into fat was my demon. It scared me. I felt worthless."

People who do this to themselves are allowing their negative thoughts to bully and control them.

Stop listening to what society (and sometimes your parents) call perfect. Stop listening to put-downs, especially if the put-downs come from YOU.

Wake up each morning and embrace who you are. Celebrate yourself with every thought, every piece of clothing you wear, every word that comes out of your mouth. You are who you are, and nobody can change that. You failed a test? Tell yourself you tried your best. Feeling put-down by something someone said? Tell yourself: "I'm perfect the way I am."

Thoughts actually need to be trained to be positive. You're in charge of them, not the other way around.

You are strong enough. Each minute is a new miracle. Each breath is a chance to start over. Celebrate the dance of life. Look at the sun and say: "I am ALIVE! I am SHINING! And I am WORTHY!"

This is life. Your life. It should be a song. "I am alive. I am alive. I am alive. I am shining. And I am worthy."

Give your future a chance. The world wants you. Rain or shine, the world needs your smile.

Dear Diary,

It has been two years since my self-discovery.

I was 15 and writing in this journal. I didn't know what it meant to be worthy. I didn't know what it felt like to smile because I was happy with myself.

But my discovery, and recovery, doesn't take away all the pain in my heart. I still feel pain when someone I care for is struggling. Sometimes, in fact, my own pain is easier.

I feel pain when I see someone cry. I feel pain when I hear about teens my age who ended their lives by drowning or chugging pills. They didn't fight the pain. They didn't give themselves a chance; they took the easy way out.

Here I am, loving life while others are crying themselves to sleep every night — perhaps wishing they didn't exist. I can't be the only one who's happy. I want to share this happiness with the world. That's why it's my mission to speak up: not for myself but for my generation.

Maybe living our worth means being able to say: "I'm beautiful". Maybe it means saying "I'm good enough" — even when we feel like shit. Perhaps it means fighting the thoughts that say: "I want out".

Being worthy requires doing everything in our power to fight pain and live our truth (even when it feels like miles away). I'm the lucky one who discovered how amazing it is to live, knowing I'm worthy. Not everyone is so lucky.

Sincerely,
Britt

Tell me a time you felt unworthy. Did your dad or mom make you feel negative towards yourself? Did your sister pick on your outfit choice. Tell me.

CHAPTER SIX
Healing

TOOL 5: End Your Attachment And Habit

I was 16 and confused. I didn't know who I was. I couldn't look myself in the mirror and say "I love myself". Instead, I said, "I hate myself".

TWO YEARS AGO...

I'm 15. I don't like the reflection in the mirror.

I'm never going to be good enough. I'll always be "the awkward child", "the shy child", "the dumb child".

Why do I have to be such a mistake?

It's too much to handle. I wish there could be a way to get rid of them.

I do know one thing that works: Food. Salt and vinegar chips ease my stress. But it's never just a few chips. It's always the entire bag. It's what helps my pain.

I don't feel good enough, so I eat. I'm ugly, so I eat. I don't get good grades, so I eat. I'm awkward, so I eat. I'm fat, so I eat. I'm stupid, so I eat. I don't fit in, so I eat.

When I wanted to run away from my problems, food took me there. The experts call this food addiction. I call it my hiding place. When you're feeling crappy, and life keeps getting worse, addictions keep you sane. Or at least we think they do.

It was the only way I knew how to be. Life kept going so fast. I didn't have a chance to sit back and find myself.

No one has power over you.

No object or thing should ever

make you feel happy,

because you are

naturally blessed.

Free yourself!

Once upon a time, I knew a guy who was in my Grade 9 Math class. He had been battling his own demons, and the pain was too hard for him to handle. He kept thinking: "I am worthless" because his dad would hit him. He began to feel as if no one loved him, and it took a big toll on him.

He didn't know what to do. Nothing seemed to take his pain away, except for one thing: Pot. Dope. Weed.

"Why do you smoke?" I asked him.

"Because my life sucks," he said. "Why do I want to be present when reality is so crappy? Smoking takes the pain away. And even if it only lasts for an hour, so what? It's better than being fully aware and present when I go home to see my dad hitting my mom."

He was right. Reality can really suck.

What happens when you want to stop the thing you're most attached to? Does your heart pound fast? Does your hand shake? Does your head hurt? Do you feel weak mentally and physically? You might think: "I can't keep going without a hit. I need it." It might be food or new clothes or gambling or having a new boyfriend or girlfriend.

The worst part is that you don't care. Whatever it is, you want it and you'll do everything in your power to get it. You'll do whatever it takes to get the relief you crave. Addiction takes over. Addiction rules you.

So you think you can't make it without this attachment. What happens if you loosen your grip and just free it?

Often when we crave something, we're like a bird with a broken wing. A part of us is not complete. A part of us is broken. But we are the only ones who can teach ourselves to fly free again.

Food was my addiction. When I felt I wasn't accepted for who I am, I would eat. If I was happy, I'd eat. When I felt alone, I'd eat. When I was scared, I'd eat. Food became the only thing that seemed to comfort me. Eventually food became my life.

I knew I should stop, but it made me feel so good. It was the only thing that helped me forget the sadness I held inside, tucked in, away from everyone. I gained a pound, then two, then three, and then four

I noticed that my body was changing. I realized this couldn't be my life anymore. To get my wings back, I needed to let go of this habit. I heard about yoga. And thought: "it wouldn't hurt to try." When I was sad, I'd go to yoga instead of eating a full bag of salt and vinegar chips.

See how you could create positive habits?

Addiction Checklist

How many of these statements sound like you? Circle what relates to you. Or underline what doesn't resonate with you. Circle things, add a star, highlight, underline. Ask yourself: Does this sound like me? Have fun.

- ♡ Smoking dope helps me get away from my bad reality.
- ♡ Smoking cigarettes takes away stress.
- ♡ I drink my feelings away.
- ♡ Eating food removes my negative feelings.
- ♡ Having sex makes me feel loved and secure.
- ♡ Gossiping makes me feel happy.
- ♡ Being on the hockey team makes me popular. I can't let it go.
- ♡ Not eating makes me feel skinny, and I need to do that to insure I stay attractive.
- ♡ I can't stop shopping.
- ♡ I need my friends to make me feel secure.
- ♡ I can't avoid not being in a relationship.
- ♡ Meeting celebrities makes me feel cool, and I can't live without attention from my peers.
- ♡ I need to play with my Xbox.
- ♡ I need to work out.
- ♡ I need to be studying.

See: there are so many things we can become attached to. The choice is yours: are you going to let it consume you or break the habit now?

Did you know that having romantic relationships is one of the biggest addictive habits we have? Is this your addiction? Do any of these statements sound like you?

- I need somebody to make me feel happy with myself.
- I am afraid of rejection.
- I need to feel loved, no matter who it is.
- I'd rather be with someone than no one, even if it's a person who is bad for me.
- I crave sex.
- I need to be in a relationship.
- Being with someone makes me feel special and wanted.

People attachment: "I need him!"

If this is you, listen carefully.

You don't need his touch. You need "a" touch. Anyone available will do. You don't want your bed to be empty tonight. An empty bed scares you.

You can't be anything without him (or her). Being alone makes you feel unattractive. So you make it your mission to find someone who will keep you company. You won't be alone tonight.

"How do you rebuild yourself?" a girl once asked me. "I'm just a bad person," she said, "and I'm ashamed of myself. It's exhausting, just carrying around guilt and negativity."

"What's weighing you down?" I asked.

"Honestly," she answered, "I've done so many things I'm not proud of. I've lied, slept around, stole. It would take me forever to list everything."

"There's a core to all our problems," I said. "Think about why you sleep around, for instance."

"Well, first," she answered, "I'm a really like, *really* jealous person. I'm very insecure about a lot of things (my body, mostly), and I seek attention. I'll send guys nude pictures of myself. They'll say, instantly, Wow! Nice body!' and I need to hear that. I need attention."

If this is your addiction, remember: You don't need a guy, a girl, or anyone to make you feel good, because let's face it: You already are amazing just the way you are.

Any time you feel lonely, just tell yourself: "I **don't** need to be in a relationship to feel good about myself."

Celebrity attachment

Did you know attachments towards celebrities is a huge addiction?

Ask yourself:
- Do you act like yourself around a celebrity?
- Do you show all your friends pictures of the meet-and-greet?
- Do you post it all over social media so others can see?
- Do you take every chance to meet them?

Now ask yourself: Does this sound like me?

From Taylor Swift to Justin Bieber, travelling from one state to another. Why? People do it to meet a celebrity and have their own five minutes of fame.

I understand the need, just as I understand the need to fit in and be respected by the popular kids. One way to do this for some people is to travel long distances so they can have their pictures taken and then post them on social media. Five minutes with Justin Beiber = 100 likes on Instagram.

They think that once people see who they've met, they're no longer a loser. Now they think they will be liked, accepted, and popular. The emptiness goes, and so does the pain. But of course, it doesn't last and so they have to make it happen again. And they chase after another celebrity.

Is this you? If you feel that you always need a picture with your favorite celebrity, maybe you should start thinking of it as an addiction.

Try using this affirmation: "No celebrity has the power to make me feel good enough. I am better than enough on my own."

Workout attachment

Ask yourself:
- Do you act like yourself around people who find you attractive?
- When you work out, do you do it because it makes you feel healthy and happy?
- When you work out, is there a thought in the back of your mind that says: "If I gain more abs, I'll get more girls"? Are you doing it for you, or for them?
- Does working out make you feel good?
- Do you want to look like others rather than yourself?

Then ask yourself: Does this sound anything like me?

Most guys could relate to this addiction, but so can girls. I workout, it's my routine, but I do it for myself. It's become a positive habit.

This part is particularly for those who workout to gain attention from others.

Try to remember: the key to impressing a girl is to be real and to be original. How many times have you walked by another boy your age and noticed how muscular his body is? You notice how the girls pay attention to him. And you think: "I want that. I want girls to notice me and think I am hot."

There's a core to everyone's problems, a reason why you feel the need to work out to the extreme. You don't feel good enough. And that one-hour workout turns into another hour, and then another, until it consumes your life.

You probably never know how many girls might have already glanced at you from afar.

Maybe you were told you're fat, and now you make it your mission never to feel fat again. Lifting weights, running on the treadmill, doing 100 pushups all for what? For some girl to look at you?

I'm all into working out, eating organic foods and being healthy, but not if it consumes my entire life, I don't do it for approval, that's the difference.

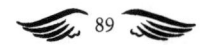

If this is your habit, tell yourself: "No attention can make me feel good about myself, because I am better than enough on my own. I go to the gym to feel strong in my body, and healthy. I release my attachment today."

Your addiction is **not** so much addiction as attachment. Habits ease our emotional pain. Through life, people leave, people change, and people grow. We realize that nothing lasts forever. We can try our hardest to hold onto the things that make us feel alive. So what do we do? We become attached to objects or people or ideas. We know obsessing over a car or a new shirt can't really hurt us. They can get lost, but it only takes a bit of money to replace them.

Our attachments are our weaknesses. How do you break free from this madness? How do you escape from this time that's like a dark, gloomy winter night? Just like when there's a snowstorm, you might dream of standing in warm sunshine with your feet in the ocean. Releasing your attachments feels similar to that.

You are the one who can make yourself happy, not your friend, not a drug, or a car, or food, or a person: only yourself.

TURN THIS ADDICTION INTO A MEDITATION.

Every time you feel like you need the drug, the food, the thing, the person, breathe in a little deeper, notice how you feel. Shaky, nauseous, dizzy? Breathe into that sensation.

Ask yourself: "How do I feel?" Overeaters: Are you really hungry or is it your mind speaking to you, tell you to eat because it's programmed that way? Smokers: breathe deeper. Let yourself feel how your mind can affect your body. Breathe in deeper when you feel the dizziness come upon.

Every single time an urge comes along, breathe, breathe, breathe, feel how it affects your body, mind and soul.

Think of yourself as a beautiful bird trapped in a cage, and the only thing you've ever wanted is to be free. Your attachment is keeping you from flying high and flutter like a butterfly. Who you are in this exact moment is the person, right now, who can stop feeding the addiction. It's time to let go of all the things that hold you back.

Step into the world where nothing has control over you. You're free and not trapped in some dark alley.

I once read "everything we want or have isn't really ours"-
From attachment to detachments, when we learn it's never been ours, it doesn't belong to us, it becomes easier to let go.
Hmm ..Tell me a time you couldn't let go of something. What was it exactly?

Habits

Change is a good thing.

Change your days! Do something different every day.

Keep in mind that habits can either make you or break you.

What a nightmare, doing the same thing every hour, every day, right? A habit is like constantly walking down the same road, seeing the same people on your way, looking at the same things, every day a repeat of the day before.

Habits are our friends at good times, our enemies during the bad times. But they can rule our lives. They can keep us in a box.

An ex-smoker picks up another cigarette; an alcoholic takes one more shot; a girl chews her lip; a man bites his nails; a drug addict pops another pill.

Habits can help you or ruin you. You have them to give you a few minutes of happiness. When you're told to change your habits, your first reaction is: "But I CAN'T!"

Before I went to high school, I was scared because I figured going into "the big school" meant not slacking off on my homework ever and changing the way I am used to being. Everything did change. My life was completely different from elementary school.

If you could make your weekdays just like your weekends, would you? The word "change" scares most of us. It leaves us to second-guess the way things will be.

"What if" is scary, too. "What if this happens?" "What if that happens?" But if you allowed the word "change" to be something positive, the question "What if?" might take on a happy meaning.

This is my life

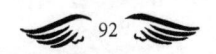

I wake up at 8 a.m. seven days a week. Monday. Tuesday. Wednesday. Thursday. Friday. I have school. During these weeks I have people staring at me, judging me, giving me dirty looks. Morning after morning, it is the same.

The only different thing I do from day to day is to wear a different outfit. I eat the same breakfast. I talk to the same people at school. I take the same road to get to school. I see the same teachers. Day after day, a repeat.

Boring!

Weekends come and it's different. We get the freedom to do whatever we want. I like to change up my two days than I'm off school.

You can't control what happens, but you can change the way you react. You can't change the fact that school is something you have to do, but you can change how you react, right?

While you are at school, try talking to different people. Perhaps you will walk in different pathways and bring up different conversations.

Someone once said to me: "If you sit with a different group during school every day for a month, then it won't feel strange."

The first time we change our daily lives and do something different than our usual routine, it feels really strange and weird. However, if we just sit and speak to different people at school for a month or so, we won't have to think about it. So habits can change, just like that. It's easy to get attached, but it's easy to get out of it, too. All you have to do is to change things up.

Habits can be positive or negative.

Positive examples:
- Thinking positively
- Exercising regularly for good intentions
- Planning ahead
- Having respect for others every day
- Making regular acts of kindness maybe even put them into a schedule.

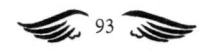

Negative examples:
- Gossiping
- Over - or under - eating
- Drinking, smoking
- Bullying
- Thinking negatively
- Feeling inferior to or better than others
- Blaming others for our problems

My positive habit is Yoga. I exercise when I am upset. When I am mad or angry, I listen to soulful, uplifting music that always seems to calm me down.

If everyone around us had positive habits, we wouldn't feel as though our world was crashing down. We wouldn't feel alone.

Negative habits have the ability to destroy us. They can turn us into monsters and make us the kind of people we never wanted to be.

Try doing three things.

You might see a transformation in your life. I did, and suddenly everything changed.

1 Admit to your habit. Don't avoid it. Be honest at least to yourself. You don't need to share this with anyone.

2 Make an effort. If you want to see results, right here and right now take action. Change your habit into something positive. Don't just sit in your room waiting for things to change. I did that, and it never worked. Waiting for a miracle without any effort is like saying you will fly tomorrow. It's impossible. So go for it. Change things up.

3 Have faith in yourself. This is a time to acknowledge that you are good enough. This is a moment to sit back and reflect on your life. You are on this world for a reason. You are meant to shine. After making such an incredible effort to see results, this is a time when you sit back and say: "I did it! I put effort, energy and time into changing my habits, and now I see results. Now I have faith in myself."

Remember the boy who never thought he was good enough? The one who kept smoking pot to ease his pain? He was right about that. It did ease his pain for about an hour at a time. Then reality hit and all his feelings and memories came back.

He never thought he could heal himself. He didn't imagine that he could reach as high as the sky to find the light inside him. He thought miracles only happened in fiction or fairy tales.

But then he met someone who changed his perspective, and now he believes miracles do happen.

You just need to find the right people to believe in you and help you free yourself. His mentor told him: "Each smoke you inhale is one day less you have in this world. What are you going to do when smoking weed turns into snorting coke? You'll overdose and leave your mom to live a life on her own. Nobody will protect her, and you will leave her. She will fight her demons on her own. Your spirit will be up there with the rest. Your body will be buried under the ground. And you will leave without completing any purpose whatsoever."

The man paused and continued: "Is that what you want?"

"No," he told his mentor. "That is not what I want."

The same thing goes with you, is that what you want? Do you want you addiction, attachments, habits take over your entire future?

Tell me one negative habit you wish to change.
Examples: Do you smoke daily? Do you drink constantly? Do you over eat?
Do you under eat?

Tell me one positive habit that effectively works for you.
Examples: Do you workout? Do you practice yoga? Do you go on a daily jog? Do you take a cold shower in the morning to wake yourself up? Do you eat healthy nutrition that's right for your body?

CHAPTER SEVEN
Belonging

TOOL 6: Find Your Place In Life

5 YEARS AGO

I'm turning 13 in a few months. Maybe Wesley will like me and not view me as Sam's little sister. Just a few more months and I become a woman. 13.

It's 6 a.m. and I have to get up to watch my sister's karate tournament. Otherwise I'd NEVER be up this early.

I get up before my Mom comes into my room and yells: "Brittany. Britt. BRITT. Wake up now. We leave in 20 minutes!"

Sometimes I wonder if she knows I can hear her. She doesn't need to yell.

My dad won't get mad at me because I'm ready before everyone else in my family.

Note to self: Never annoy or piss Dad off during karate tournaments. It's his happy place where he feels his best. He gets anxious and rude at the same time, even though it isn't his tournament- Something I'll never understand.

So I stay away from him. Actually, I stay away from everybody. I don't want the attention or spotlight to be on me. I pull out my phone and sit beside my mom. She is quiet like me, so I know if I stay near her, nobody will try to speak to me.

My sister is the next one to do her thing: her kata, or routine. The spotlight is on her. Cameras are taping her, and people are cheering for her.

This man sitting in the row behind me just poked my shoulder. "Is that your sister over there?" he asks. I look back. Who the heck is he?

"Yeah, she is," I say. He continues to talk, and he's annoying me.

"Well, she's wonderful," he ends up saying.

I never get jealous or want to be someone else, because I am used to living in a separate world than everyone else. I'm sort of closed off from people. I don't feel average. I always feel different.
All of a sudden I feel this emotion. I think I'm going to cry. No, I can't. Not here, not where everyone can see me. I run to the washroom.

"Mom, I'll be back," I say quickly. "Need to pee."

The emotion passes like a wave. Tears are dripping down my face. I have to be strong. I wipe the tears and say one more time: "Brittany, get yourself back up. Don't show people your weakness."

I look at myself in the mirror and I wonder: When will I start feeling like I belong? When will I know who I am?

I walked miles and miles to find out who I was. I kept asking: what keeps my heart pumping? What keeps my eyes open? What settles my heart? I had to walk through valleys, mountains and jungles to find my passion.

When I look directly into babies' clear, pure eyes, everything inside me hopes they will find their place in life. I hope they will have the best childhood experiences. I hope they will have the best high school experience ever, and find lifelong friends who last forever.

Haven't you looked at babies and wished they wouldn't have to experience the same struggles, obstacles and challenges of finding themselves in this world?

Most of us have found it difficult to find a place, to feel a sense of home, a sense of security. We all just want a place in this world, a place where we can say: I belong here.

Every day I watch people (but not in a creepy way) as they get into their cars, walk into their homes, shop in grocery stores or at the mall. They all seem as though they belong somewhere.

From my perspective, they fit in this world. They're perhaps working at a job that brings out their greatest passion. Perhaps they have a family who loves them, or they have great friends. Or maybe they don't. I'm just assuming.

I looked closer; and everything I thought was a false assumption. I noticed the sadness upon people's faces. Everybody wants to feel average, they do everything in their power to become "perfection", though it never works. We are all NOT average. We all struggle with finding a place of belonging.

Everybody has a perk of sadness, not always a spark of happiness.

People don't always have it all together even if they seem as though they do. Everyone gets confused. Everyone gets lost and feels alone at times. Why do you think people have hobbies and activities? Go to the gym? Play hockey? Go to dance classes?

They do it so they can take an hour or so and just enjoy the moment. If they're having a bad day, they can sweat it out on the treadmill. Where they get the chance to let their energy out.

READY TO FIND YOUR PLACE IN LIFE?

Do you wonder: Where do I belong? How often does that question go unanswered? We don't always know what career path to take or what friends to talk to. We don't know where our place is.

I always felt different from others. I wasn't like my sister. I wasn't like my dad. I wasn't like my mom, either. I never felt as though I belonged. I sometimes wondered: was I adopted?

Sometimes I'd actually search the house for clues that would tell me I was adopted. Then one time I was in my parents' office. I was going through everything – opening every cupboard, taking piles of paper off the desk, and so on. I was making a huge mess.

My mom walked into the room. "What are you doing?" she asked.

Busted.

So I said it straight out. "Am I adopted?"

My mom just started laughing.

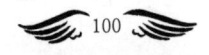

"What's so funny?" I asked.

"You look too much like your father to be adopted," she said, still laughing.

She showed me a picture of her pregnant stomach, and pictures of me at birth. But I kept thinking: This is B.S. – I'm adopted.

But I wasn't. All this time I felt so different from everyone that I didn't think I could possibly have come from my parents. I wasted energy accusing my mother of not telling the truth.

All I needed was to find out where I belong.

Why do we change ourselves?

Maybe every night you turn on the TV and you watch Gossip Girl. Maybe you think or say out loud: "I want Blake Lively's hair" or the clothes of the character, Blair. You want all the things you don't have. You want to look like them, act like them, dress like them. You want to be their friends. So you change yourself to be like them.

Sometimes we do this to be accepted, but most of the time we do it because we don't know ourselves, so we live in other people's shadows. We become followers.

If this is you, don't worry. There's nothing wrong with you. I lived in my sister's shadow for most of my life, wishing and hoping one day I'd be her. Then I lived in my friends' shadows, dressing and acting like them. None of it was ever me. It was an act.

My sister at 6
She was talkative. She had found Karate. She made friends.

I was three. I was shy and without a voice, still. There was a part of me that wanted to be her so badly. But how could that be if I was silent? I thought: When I turn 6, I will be like her.

I turned 6
I still had no friends. I still didn't speak for myself. My wish didn't come true. I wasn't like my sister.

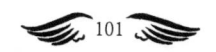

My sister was 9 by now. She was still doing Karate. It didn't just become her hobby. It was more. Everyone seemed to think it would be her path in life now.

I thought: Maybe when I turn 9, I'll find a hobby the way she did. And I'll be like her.

I turned 9
I was speaking; I had been for two years. I was shy.
My sister was 12 by now. She made even more friends. Karate was her life, not just her passion. She had school friends and Karate friends.
I thought: When will I feel like I belong and find friends who become a big part of my life? Maybe when I'm 12 I'll be like her.

I turned 12
I didn't have any passion about any activity. My parents put me into dance classes, hoping it's where I would fit in. But after awhile they realized I wasn't dancing because it excited me. I was dancing because I had nothing better to do.

My dad thought maybe I might enjoy Karate. My sister loved it, so why wouldn't I? He signed me up. I didn't like it. I pretended I did for awhile, because I wanted to belong somewhere. But Karate, like dance, just wasn't my passion.

My sister was 15
She had boys chasing her. She was beautiful. She had a great body. She had many friends. She was popular. She was still very successful at Karate.

Of course I wanted that for myself. So I told myself: Maybe when I turn 15 I'll be like her.

I turned 15
Things started getting worse. I had "popular" friends. For awhile it made me feel as though I did belong.

Then everything changed. My world crashed. My life shattered like broken glass flying in different directions. It was so painful.

I decided my friends at the time weren't the right ones for me and I had to stop looking around to find out where I belonged. I had to start looking within myself.
Sometimes you find your place in life when your world comes crashing down in front of you. There's a word for that. It's called an awakening.

At 15, I still didn't know where I belonged. If someone asked me: "What do you want to do after high school?" I had no clue. I couldn't even think of an answer. Nothing excited me. Nothing. I just kept feeling as though I didn't belong. I thought I'd never find "my people": friends who could understand and relate to me.

Try to wake up every day thinking that you're glad to be alive because today you're going to do what excites you. Maybe you're going to spin class, or to play hockey, or to dance or yoga class.

Passion should drive you to the hobby, not the other way around. Try different things to find what you like. Keep your mind open.

Every morning, ask yourself: "Who am I?" Every night, decide to find where you belong. Eventually your answer will be right. It will come in time, all upon 'divine timing'.

Right place, right time, right moment.

Nothing is impossible. YOU are possible.

If you could be anything in this world, what do you think it would be? The answer might not come today or tonight or tomorrow. But keep asking.

Children are told that dreaming is important. They're encouraged to doodle, paint, and imagine. So why isn't it important for teenagers? Instead we hear: "You're too old for that", or "You're acting immature", or "How old are you? Two?"

Imagine your own world where you can be anything. Where you can talk to anyone you want. Where nothing gets in your way. Feel how unstoppable you are. You feel light, not heavy, because there is no tension.

I always used to think I would never find my tribe, my people – friends who completely understand me. I asked and asked: Universe; Higher Power; God; anyone listening to me: Please bring like-minded people into my life.

Days went by. Weeks flew by. Time kept going on. And not once did I find any like-minded people.

I started to think that maybe I'd just be alone forever, without friends. And then one day I met an awesome woman named Judy. I was at an inspirational event. It was about how anything is possible. Actually, it was called "Im. Possible", and that's where I learned that the word itself means *"I'm possible"*.

Judy came up to me and introduced herself. I knew instantly that we were alike. She told me about her book that just came out: "Life Purpose Playbook." I was so excited. I thought: "She's absolutely a like-minded person."

We connected. We shared numbers. That night I got a text from her.

"Come to a picnic with me on Saturday," she said. "You'll meet my community of people who want to change the world too." Without thinking twice, I wrote back: "Heck, YES."

I went to the picnic and saw all kinds of wonderful people. There were many things to discuss: How we can change the world. How we like yoga.

I met some people that I've stayed connected to. Since I know my place in this life, people just like myself are vibrating similar energy; similar morals and personalities. My tribe is forming, one by one.

I do belong.

What do you enjoy most?

School is my prison cell

School is not for everyone – it wasn't for me. I didn't find a place where I belonged.

What is school? Is it an institute where we sit for hours in a small classroom, bored out of our minds? Yep.

Doesn't everybody say this? "Go to school. Get high marks. Get a good job. Go to university. Get a degree. Marry the next person who comes into your life. Have two kids."

Isn't that what society tells us to do?

We do what seems to be average in order to be an ordinary person.

"Good morning, Mom," I say. "Guess where I'm going today?"

Where, Sweetie?" she answers.

I'm thinking whatever I'm about to say will either make my mom mad or laugh. Whichever one it will be, I can't wait to see her reaction.

I say: "I'm going to prison."

Poor mom. Her mouth opens.

"What are you talking about? Prison? No way. Don't be silly."
I laugh!

"No, Mom, it's a different kind of prison. I won't be dressed in an orange suit or locked behind bars. It's actually called school."

But I will be locked from being who I am.

"School is my prison," I say.

Why aren't teachers educating us to be ourselves? Why aren't they educating us on life skills? What kind of world are we living in when our thoughts aren't smart enough, when we are defined by marks?

In my tenth grade, one of my teachers told me he was retiring in a month, and he was going to tell me something important.

"In my second year of teaching," he said, "I was 27, and I had a boy who never came to class. I thought he was skipping class to go out and smoke and drink with his friends. I assumed he was a stoner. But I was wrong. I guess teachers assume things. We do favor kids. And it's not right. While I was thinking this kid was smoking his lungs out, he was actually downtown auditioning for an acting role. He was pursuing his dream.

"Maybe if I asked him where he'd been, that would have solved everything. But I didn't, because I thought every kid came to class every day to get perfect marks. But this kid, he'd rather spend his days living his passion, instead of being told what to do or think. Here in school, we are supposed to educate students to go to university, and to follow everything society says; but I'm starting to believe it's not true.

"Be yourself. Live your passion. I turned on the TV the other day, and that boy had grown into a man – living his passion of acting.

"He told me: 'School is a game'. I think you might agree."

How many times have teachers made you feel worthless? You didn't get a good mark on a test, so you went home and cried. You didn't know the answer to the question your teacher asked you, and it annoyed you all day.

Don't be average. Being average sucks. Follow your dreams. Don't let educators stop you.

Life is about freedom. Don't be locked up in an institution for the rest of your life if that's not where your passion is.

Do you feel school is locking you, like a prison?

CHAPTER EIGHT
Infinite Possibilities

We can create anything.
We can become anything we really want.
When somebody says, "It's impossible"
Say: "No! Anything is possible".
The word itself means: "I'm possible".

This is called: The gift of manifestation

It's the power to manifest a thought or intention into your life. You have the power to go anywhere, to have anything, to do everything you hope for. That is if you believe in it. Can you? Maybe I should ask you: "Will you? Will you believe that your dream- intention will manifest into your life all on perfect timing?"

My grandfather has always told me: "When people say, 'It's impossible', I like saying back to them: 'Anything is possible until you can prove otherwise'."

Zaida Lorrie's words will always stick with me. It's what I believe in and how I choose to live my life. Anything is possible.

This is Zaida Lorrie's story:

"School isn't my thing. I don't do good. I don't find it interesting. I wanted to be a 'somebody'. I wanted to accomplish the one thing that even my parents didn't think was possible – to become one of the best jockeys of my time. Could I do it? Was it possible? People kept telling me, 'Lorrie, stop dreaming. It's impossible for you to become the world's best jockey!'"

Well, do you think he did it? He didn't start training at an early age, as most jockeys do.

"I went home one night," he continued, "and thought to myself, this is my passion! I'm done with school. I will pursue this passion and train every day to become the best. I won't stop now or listen to anyone who doubts me. This is my dream, I thought, and I will chase it."

Zaida Lorrie dropped out of high school to become the best jockey of his time. He isn't your average person. He trained every day, woke up seeing every sunrise, and trained all the way to dawn until it was dark outside.

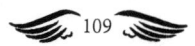

"I fell off the horse so many times," he recalls. "I broke my arm. I broke my leg. I had a lot of injuries, and many barriers got in the way. But I never once allowed these things to stop me. I recovered and I told myself: 'I'll do better this time', and when I fell, I kept telling myself: 'Next time I will do better'."

Zaida Lorrie is a true legend. He had a lot of fire in him. He fell, and he got up.

"I have such a love and passion for the horse," he said. "When you're riding, it's you and the horse, and you get into your own little world, escaping from reality. You feel the wind blowing in your face. You feel the sun shining above you, and your body moves to the bumps and roads the horse takes you to. It's freedom that I needed for so long, and the horse gave me exactly that – the freedom to go places where nobody could annoy me or push my buttons."

There were two of the world's best jockeys who mentored Zaida Lorrie: Avelino Gomez and Sandy Hawley.

"If you want to be the best," they told him, "the first thing to remember is this: Never let anyone discourage you into believing you aren't a good jockey. Watch us and learn. It's the best way to do it. Watch videos, and ask questions."

Zaida proved all the people wrong. "It feels amazing to say that!" he said. "Just after a year of intense training and learning, I became a professional jockey. I rode one of the best horses, and won the races. People wanted my autograph!

"One time a kid asked me for my autograph, and I said: 'Of course, anytime!' I asked him where I should sign. He said 'Well, I don't have a paper.' I said: 'No problem. Let me find one for you.' He smiled. I came back with a paper and said: 'Here you go.' He said, 'Well, Lorrie, I don't have a pen.' So I said: 'You're a funny kid. Okay, I'll go find you one.' I came back with a piece of paper and pen. Then I signed it for him and I wrote: *'Don't ever let anyone stop you from chasing your dreams'.*"

Horses became Zaida Lorrie's life. They weren't just animals to him. They were his friends. They taught him that anything is possible. His story passes on from generation to generation, to teach us that we can become anything.

Three rules:

1 Dream it.

2 Don't give up, until your dream has become your life.

3 Be grateful to yourself for all the hard work you've put into making it possible. Maybe give thanks to the 'higher source', whether it's the 'universe', G-D, or a higher power out there, make sure you give your gratitude.

You have the gift called manifestation.

We literally can become anything we want. All you need to do is direct your energy on that one vision of yours. Keep seeing it. Keep focusing. Don't say: I will... Say: It's mine. I know." When we bring confidence and knowing that your vision, dream, intention is already yours, then it TRULY becomes your life, your reality.

1) Has there ever been a time you felt like something was impossible?
2) Tell me what it is exactly you want to accomplish...
Instead of using "I want"- change the worlds to- "I am.. or I choose to be a doctor. I choose to a bestseller author. I choose to be a hockey player. I choose to be NYC Broadway performer."

CHAPTER NINE
Perception

TOOL 7: Walk The Walk

> "You never really know a man until you understand things from his point of view, until you climb into his skin and walk around in it".
>
> -HARPER LEE
> (To Kill a Mockingbird)

"Brittany is so weird. She's so stupid. She's a dumb blonde. I don't even want to be friends with her. She does weird things, like meditation. I don't like her. She's so fat. And fake."

Yep. That's what people thought of me. To them, I was fake, stupid, weird, loser, and fat. But that was their opinion. Not mine.

It's all a matter of perception.

We all have opinions. Who I am to you might be different to somebody else. Who you are to your mom might be someone different to your boyfriend. Who you are to your friends might be someone different to your grandpa. Get it?

We all have different perceptions of each other.

The gossiping, the name-calling, the mean comments: they're just people's ideas of who they think you are.

READY TO WALK THE WALK?

My mentor told me: "Brittany, I'm going to take you on a walk. I want to teach you about trust. It's called 'Walk the Walk'. But there's more to it. I'm going to blindfold you. You won't be able to see anything…"

"No way," I said. "I'll fall or – even worse – get hit by a bus."

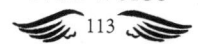

"Do you think I would let that happen?" she asked. "Trust me and you will be safe."

"Fine," I said.

She covered my eyes. I couldn't see where I was going. My nerves were on edge. But I needed to trust.
"I'm taking you down a long path," she said. "As you take each step, I want you to remember that you're not the only one bumping into detours or feeling scared about the unknown.

"Think of this path as a story. Everyone you can't see right now has a story. If you could see what they look like, you might judge them for that. You might judge them for what they believe in and what they do. You can't see the people who just walked by you, so you can't judge them by their outfits, can you?"

I thought about it. No, I couldn't judge them because I couldn't see them. All I could do was to hear footsteps, or the wind, or buses and cars driving past.

"You're right," I said. "It's a journey. They have a story. I have a story. But if I saw everything in front of me, I would most likely be judging them."

"And what you don't know," she went on, "is that what you see may not be who they are at all. Sometimes people wear masks."

It's your time to walk the walk. It's your time to get to understand the person or people you think are weird, or the people you don't like.

If there was one piece of advice I'd say to my long-gone "popular" friends, it would be this: Before you judge me, understand why I'm not like you. Take a step in my shoes. Walk the life I am living. If you can get as far as I have, maybe you will see me for the person I really am, not the person you think I am.

Maybe if my "popular" friends got to understand me, they would see all the accomplishments I've had, all the people I've touched. And they would see how strong I am – behind the mask.

Behind their perception, they would see *me*.

The "self" we show people at school during social interactions or math class is different from the "self" we really are. We go home and shut the doors to our reality.

We hurt others so no one will see the real story. But everyone deals with crap. Everyone. We are all more alike than we think.

Can you imagine living in a world where everyone you meet, everyone you know, has, let's say, the same skin disease as you? Sounds a little crazy, but think about it: All people from all walks of life, their bodies covered with red, infected wounds. They're in pain. They're yelling. You wouldn't be able to touch anyone because they'd scream: "It HURTS!"

There'd be no interaction. No intimacy. No love or connection. Just fear. Just anger.

If this was our reality and if every single person in the world was experiencing such a disease, everyone would understand each other. They would know about the physical hurt. They would understand how it hurts emotionally, too, never to be touched.

This is perception.

You would be walking each other's walk. You would be living each other's pain. You would have the same struggle as your neighbor. We would all be one.

Okay, so we don't all have a skin disease. But we do have pain. We all know what it's like to feel inadequate. We all struggle in some way.

I hear this all the time at school:
- She's such a loser.
- She's fat.
- That outfit doesn't match.
- She's such a wannabe.
- He's stupid.
- She's anorexic.
- He's a man whore.

- He's such a jerk.
- She needs to stop eating so much.
- How can such a hot guy go out with such an ugly girl?
- I hate his laugh.
- What a loser.
- They're such slobs.
- She dresses like she's in the 60s.
- I'm gonna smash your face in your locker.

Why do we do it? When we say all these things, all we're doing is giving someone a reason to cry. We're giving someone a reason to ask: "Why am I alive?" And: "Why does no one at school like me?"

Most of us have said something mean to another person. Most of us have at least felt it or seen it.

There are three kinds of people: the bully, the ones whose hearts are broken, and the ones who are watching and laughing.

When we're in pain, we think gossiping about others will somehow ease that pain. But it does the opposite, and it creates a bigger pain for someone else.

Children accept their little buddies for who they are. If your buddy falls off a swing and hurts himself, it hurts you, and you cry, too.

Now when someone falls, you laugh at them. When you were little, you had beautiful eyes of wonder and acceptance. Later on, life happened. You grew up. And now you're not crying with your friend. You're laughing at him.

School is the one place where we're supposed to feel safe. And yet all I hear are these awful comments about people – and about me. They don't know me. They don't know the first thing about me.

How many kids cry themselves to sleep because mom is always drunk or on drugs? How many are getting slapped by their mom's new boyfriend? How many of us know the stories of others? We don't, because most of the time we don't see what's really happening in their lives.

We never walk the walk. We don't take the time to understand someone. If we got to know the person we were repeating all the rumors about, we might feel pretty bad.

I asked one guy, a teen but not an average one, what his story was.
"My name is Dylan," he said. "I'm new to this school. I'm not your average-looking boy, as you can probably tell. I don't have muscles like Nick in my math class does. I know I mumble my words, and everyone makes fun of that."

He told me about the time his English teacher singled him out and asked him to introduce himself to the class.

He was nervous about it. Really nervous. That was why he had come to this school, to get away from his old school, where everyone laughed at him when he had to speak in front of the class.

He tried, but all that came out were stutters. He could hear the laughing and whispers in the back of the classroom. He heard someone whisper, loudly: "He's so weird! Did you hear his voice?"

He was about to give up. But all of a sudden, out of nowhere, this guy named Justin stood up. Justin looked like one of the popular kids. He had this great hockey jacket and he looked like a body builder.

"Hey, Dylan," Justin said, "Ignore these immature girls who are laughing at you. They don't know anything about respect or kindness. They don't know or care that everyone has a story. I guess their parents never taught that being judgmental is a very bad habit. Anyway, it's nice to meet you, bro. You can sit beside me, if you want to."

Dylan was shocked. Did that jock just invite him, the loser, to come sit with him? He was in awe of Justin's courage.

Dylan's story inspires me each day to be like Justin and never again to be pulled into gossiping and negative, mean opinions.

No more bullying. No more hurting. Love only.

Have you ever heard that once you are forgiven you are free?

If you have bullied someone, ask for his or her forgiveness. If you are the one who has been bullied, forgive the person who bullied you.

Even bullies have stories. Maybe they, most especially, have stories. Bullies have usually been bullied themselves. You can be sure there's a painful reason behind their mean actions.

Does this sound anything like you?
Highlight, underline, circle or put a heart or star beside the statements that sound like you. Have fun with this – and come a few steps closer to finding out more things about yourself.

- ♡ I will never forgive them. They are hateful and mean.
- ♡ I will never forget what they said.
- ♡ He (or she) ruined my life.
- ♡ I'm not forgiving them unless they apologize first.
- ♡ I never forgive anyone. Why should I when I'm right and they're wrong?
- ♡ I forgive because I believe everyone deserves a second chance.
- ♡ Nobody's perfect. I always forgive.

Imagine yourself walking down your school hallway and not being pushed into the locker. Imagine walking past the cafeteria without being laughed at. Imagine a whole day at school without being picked on, gossiped about or bullied.

School would be so much better if we only just accepted each other. We wouldn't be going home miserable every day.

WHY DO THEY DO IT?

Some kids have this tape playing in their heads. It goes like this: Fat-ugly-loser-nerd-weird. Fat-ugly-loser-nerd-weird. It goes around and around and never stops. It's there at school and then when they go home, chaos breaks out. It might be a drunken mother or parents who are abusive. It might be a place where no one notices them or cares that they're alive. It might be a dysfunctional family they have to care for because no one else will.

And then, at school, some popular girl starts the tape again. Only this time it's: *"No one cares about you, you're the least popular person here, people pretend to like you but you're really just an ugly little geek who should sink down to the ground where you belong."*

This is what bullies often hear, so the bully goes first and does the name-calling before someone can do it to him or her. The bully gossips, always behind someone's back. For a moment here and there, it takes the sting out of the pain they live every day. It takes the focus off them, off the horrible things their own parents have said to them that morning, off the way other kids laughed at them. Bullies often believe they are the disgusting human beings, not the ones they're tormenting.

How can you forgive someone who hurt you and made you cry every day?

I forgave the girl who started a rumor about me. I forgave the boy who told everybody at school that I am weird. I forgave the person who told me I wouldn't be anything in this world.

It isn't easy, of course. If it was, we all would have figured it out. Forgiveness is still something I haven't fully understood yet. But I know if I start with making that change now, and end my gossiping, I will feel better about myself.

There is a story behind each person you met.

Listen to it.

Has there ever been a time you've bullied (or hurt somebody else)? How did you feel? Have you ever been hurt and bullied? How did you feel?

CHAPTER TEN
Imperfection

TOOL 8: Let Mistakes Teach You Lessons

I trusted the wrong guy.

I cheated on my girlfriend.

I failed my exam.

I should never have become friends with Sasha.

I keep making mistakes.

I'll never be good enough.

When will I stop making mistakes? When will I be perfect?

Well, maybe never. We're all imperfect. None of us excels every time we do something. We often fail. But that's okay, because it's who we are and it's what we're supposed to do.

We're supposed to find the worst guy to fall in love with. To find the meanest friends to hang out with. To make the dumbest choices about all kinds of things. Really!

That's because **mistakes teach us lessons**. They're our biggest and most important teachers.

We have heartbreaks, mean friends, bad marks and multiple mistakes. But you know what? If you take a look at the word "imperfection", and you break it apart, you'll find two words: "I'm perfect". Because we are.

READY TO LEARN FROM MISTAKES?

We might meet people and then they become the people who are our best friends: BFFL. Our best-friendship might last a month or two and then reality hits. They really aren't true friends after all. So we made a mistake. Should we accept it? Or dwell on the fact that "my so-called best friend slept with my boyfriend"?

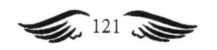

We should accept it because it's in our past now. And it has taught us that not everyone is who they say they are.

Our stories include each of our embarrassments, hurts, and mistakes; every error and every trial. But they also include our successes and triumphs.

There's a lot we don't have control over: who will break our trust. Who will spread rumors about us. But we do have control over what we will do about it, and one of those things is to accept it and move on.

Let's say your boyfriend cheats on you. And you keep saying, over and over: "I regret being with him. He's a man whore." But instead of that, say: "My story is my story. It is what it is. I choose to accept the good with the bad. I choose to accept mistakes and regrets as my teachers."

Improvement

We have the capacity to improve every single day, to become better and stronger. I was once really upset because I was getting sick and life just kept throwing bad experiences at me, one after the other. They were starting to overtake my mood.

I kept asking myself: Is it going to get any better soon? I kept trusting the wrong people or crying because he didn't like me or freaking out because I told the wrong person a secret.

"As soon as the fog clears," my mentor, Judy, said, "you will get stronger. Once your cold goes away, you'll feel better. Your immune system will get stronger; you'll be able to go out more; and life will seem brighter."

When I told her I felt unloved and how I trusted the wrong guy, and he didn't like me when I liked him, she reminded me that it was a lesson.

"Once you learn how to overcome a mistake without regret," she said, "it will improve your life. You'll feel happier."

Dear "Old" Brittany:

Just last year, you sat home every night, wishing and hoping that everything would get better. You didn't know what to do.

You just kept making mistakes. You were talking to the wrong people about the transformation that was taking place in your life. People were starting rumors about you. You put your secrets or feelings into the hands of the wrong people.

You thought you were a mistake and that you didn't deserve the life you were living. But then you found the power that is always within you if you look.

And you became the "new" Brittany. The Brittany who isn't afraid to jump into challenging situations. Who isn't afraid to make mistakes. Who sees them as teachable moments.

Thank you for the mistakes that made you cry. They made you stronger.

Sincerely,
Newly discovered Britt

There are so many famous artists, scientists, actors, models and writers who were told NO, whose work was rejected; but that didn't stop them.

- Did you know Elvis was told to return to his old job driving trucks because he didn't have any talent?
- Lady Gaga was fired by one of her first labels after only three months.
- Bill Gates dropped out of university to start a business. It failed. And then he went on to build Microsoft.
- Marilyn Munroe was told she should become a secretary because she didn't have what it took to become a model.
- Stephen King's most renowned (and first) book, Carrie, was rejected 30 times. He figured he wasn't a good enough writer and he tossed the book out. Luckily his wife believed in him and went through the trash to rescue it. Then she convinced him to submit it one more time. That thirty-first time someone said yes.

So learn from that. Don't give up.

Consciousness

I once heard somebody say: "We are one with consciousness."

I wondered what that meant. How could we be one with consciousness? I thought it was weird. But it's true.

We have the choice to be conscious of what we do because we're free to explore anything in this world. We make choices about what you see, what you do, what you have. We're free to explore love, joy, beauty and also to make mistakes. We won't grow if we don't fall.

In yoga class, the teacher told us to connect our palms in prayer pose. Then she told us, while standing, to open our left leg and to place our foot below or above our knee. I didn't realize how challenging this would be. Easy, I thought.

But I couldn't keep my balance. I fell out of the pose five or more times. "You don't have to be afraid of falling," the teacher said. "When you fall out of a pose that just means your body is learning how to get stronger. One day you'll be able to do it. So keep falling. It's like life. You fall; you make mistakes; but they all teach you to be strong, to be yourself."

A YEAR AGO.

I thought Nicole was supposed to be my best friend. I have told her everything, whether it was about what guy I liked or what problem I was going through. I thought she could be trusted, a true friend.

But I guess not.

"Nicole, sometimes I can feel things," I told her. "When I meet people, it's like I can see right through them. Maybe it's energy I'm feeling, or maybe I'm just good at judging character."

The look she gave me should have told me that in a week the entire school would know. I thought true friends might not always understand you, but they believe in you.

I've messed up. I trusted the wrong person.

A WEEK LATER.

The entire school is laughing at me.
"Brittany is weird," they say. "Brittany has super powers!"

I come home and cry. Nicole has won. But now, the most incredible thing has happened. Somebody on Facebook has written: "Every problem has a solution." So I've started to make a solution to my problem. Nicole told the entire school that I'm weird, and I have a choice. I can cry, or I can decide not to take it personally.

I'm no longer feeling sorry for myself. I have learned. Not everyone is who they say they are. Actions prove more than words.

I will do better next time. I will learn to stay in that difficult pose in yoga. I will be a better friend. Life is about making a mess, making a fuss, making a noise, making mistakes and making the best out of everything.

*Tell me a time you felt like everything you tried to do something, it always came back with a no- decline'. Have you ever tried to be perfect?
If so, how did that end up for you?*

CHAPTER ELEVEN
Kindness

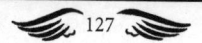

TOOL 9: Be Kind

One night before I went to sleep, I asked myself: "What does it mean to be a kind and compassionate person?"

And then, when I woke up, I remembered receiving an answer through my dream. Crazy, right?

MY DREAM...

There was a 25-year-old rich man who lived in a mansion. He had tons of money. He could buy anything in the world.

"How can I become more successful?" he asked the universe.

There was no answer. He remembered what some famous inspirational speakers have said: "What you think attracts your present reality. It's the Law of Attraction."

Was the answer right in front of his eyes?

One cold snowy night in winter, there was a knock on the door. The man opened it, and there stood a 16-year-old boy. Despite the cold, the boy was only wearing a thin shirt.

"Can I trouble you for water and something to keep me warm?" the boy asked. "A blanket, perhaps?"

The rich man gave the boy water. He gave him some left over food and a blanket, too.

"I can't let this boy go back out there," he said to himself. "If he dies, it will be my fault."

Did part of him want to change his life? To give the boy a second chance at life?

As the boy started to leave, the man stopped him.

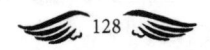

"No!" he said. "I can't let you go out there. It's too cold!" He motioned for the boy to come back in. "I have many empty rooms," he continued. "You can stay here as long as you like. You'll get food. Clean bed. And a shower."

The boy's face lit up. His expression said: Somebody cares about me!

"God bless you," he said. "Thank you!"

That was one act of kindness, but it saved the lives of two different people: the one who was helped, and the one who did the helping.

That man who asked the universe how he could be more successful got his answer. To be successful requires being kind. You can have all the money in the world and not be truly successful.

The man did have endless amounts of money. But he had spent it on things. Stuff. Possessions. Now he used it to give a young stranger a chance at life. The man had developed a golden heart.

That's the way my dream ended.

READY TO BE KIND TO YOURSELF AND OTHERS?

The people I look up to always say: "What you do to others comes back to you."

I live up to this. Be kind to others, and you will be happy. It's like the feeling you get when you give a homeless man a burger. You see his smile and you know you've helped him get through another day. It's a beautiful feeling.

Be nice to others and the world will be nice to you. If you're a care-giver, one who always gives, you need to give *yourself* a bit of kindness. Treat yourself to a spa day or a football game.

I have been asking: How can I serve more? How can I help more?

One day the answer came to me.

If you take your talents and you use them to do kind things for others – without expecting a price in return, you're serving humanity. You're

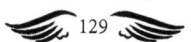

contributing to the greater good of the world.
You are the same as any stranger who walks by you. Everyone is ONE. Every person you know is the same as you, part of you. What is inside of others is inside you. If you give kindness to others, you automatically give kindness to yourself.

I enjoy helping people, so what am I doing right now? I'm writing to help you.

Use your talents to help others. Are you a painter? Paint a beautiful picture and give it to a children's hospital. Do you have extra clothing? Give it to a nearby shelter. See someone in a bad mood? Give them a smile.

Open your heart. Let go of your busy life for a few hours and do something kind for someone else. Show others that they're not alone.

Their fight, your fight, our fight. Same thing.

Tell me a time you received love. How did it feel when somebody gave you their kind deed? Have you ever went out of your way to help somebody out? If so, how did you feel?

CHAPTER TWELVE
Trust

TOOL 10: Trust Your Inner Spark

Do you trust yourself?

I don't trust my friends.
I keep secrets to myself.
I listen to the bad thoughts in my mind.
I don't trust myself, so I live off other people's opinions.
I don't trust myself.

Does this sound anything like you?

June 14, 2015

I keep thinking to myself: Why do I always say No to every single guy who asks me out on a date?

Maybe it comes down to trust issues. Will he break my heart? Will he lean in or try to kiss me before I'm ready? Will that make me feel uncomfortable? Do I trust myself to make right decisions?

I guess this trust thing is really about me. About how I can't trust myself — and therefore I can't trust others. I keep saying no to every guy, and who knows? This guy could have been a great friend, or that guy could have been a nice boyfriend. Maybe lots of good things could have happened, but I blocked the opportunity.

I decide to call my lovely mentor, Emily. She always seems to have the right answer. She always seems able to guide me.

"Hey, Britt," she says when she answers. "Everything okay?"

She knows something is "off". She knows from my voice. Damn, she's good!
"Actually, it's not," I say. "Today a guy asked me out for coffee, and I said No again. Why do I always do that? Why do I push people away? Everyone who wants my friendship gets pushed away eventually. Every boy who wants my attention is told No.

Why oh why do I do this?
Emily says: "There are two things happening here. One is good. One is a habit you should break. You might have said no to the boy because you've trusted your inner voice, and maybe your intuition was telling you that boy isn't someone you should hang out with."

And the other thing, she says, is that I don't trust myself. "You think you're not good enough for any guy to love you. You think you're not deserving of love, right? You fear what will happen. Will he push you into doing anything you're not comfortable doing? This may also be your intuition telling you not to see him."

I think about that. She's right. The guys I said No to all gave me creepy vibes. So yes, my intuition has told me not to.

But this time I said no because my intuition told me to go — and I went against it.

This feeling reminds me of a spark, a kind of inner spark, talking to me.

"If I can't trust myself," I ask Emily, "will I never be able to trust anyone else?"

"Let me tell you this," answers Emily. "Always say this in the morning, or when you're unsure of the future: 'How could I be more present for myself today?' There's an affirmation that always helps me to trust myself and my life, and it goes like this: 'I trust that life will provide me with everything I need and want'."

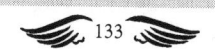

When was the last time you felt the beat of your heart, and trusted the inner spark that is in yourself, and in all of us?

Ask yourself this: "Do I trust myself enough to make the right choices, to listen to my intuition when it tells me not to do something?" Tell me what came up; do you trust yourself or not?

Maybe trust after all- is something we choose to do. Maybe it's a life-changing decision.

Our high inner walls guard us from opening our hearts. They stop us from living in the moment, because we fear something that hasn't even happened yet. *Will he hurt me? Will he cheat on me? Will she like me?* This is something I need to learn: not to let my past define my present. I fear rejection – *When he gets to know the real me, he won't like what he sees* – but I can't let that be the reason why I don't trust. It can't be the reason I say No to every person who comes into my life.

Lack of trust hardens your heart. And it builds walls that are hard to take down. I guess it happens because we are in so much pain. It's like we fight our inner sparks.

Have you ever had a feeling that is really strong, but you don't listen to it? And then you regret not listening to it because something bad happened? And you think, I could have prevented that. You fought your high inner spark – your intuition.

This is a story about a girl who doesn't trust. She is 17, in Grade 11. She had learned trust is not something she can do. So she thinks: Trust nobody.

Her mother told her to always be aware of the people around her because there are very bad people in this world. From day one she learned never to trust.

What made it worse was that it seemed her mother was right. During middle school, she heard mean words. Secrets got out. People called her names. She knew from experience, and not just from her mother's words, that she couldn't trust anyone.

She had a unique angelic quality and pure blue eyes. But she stopped smiling. She started wearing only black. She put on heavy makeup. She was scared, frightened, and hurt.

Slowly, she closed herself off from the world and the people she loved. Ugly words directed at her, name-calling, changed her.

"Trust is like a paper," she says. "Once it's torn, it can't be undone."

Do you think she'll be able to trust again?

Yes. Anything broken can be filled with love once again. Like this girl, we have all had times that make us think we can't trust others and ourselves. We think: How can trust be possible when everyone has broken their promises to me? How is it possible to trust myself when all I ever do is break the rules myself and make wrong choices? How can I trust someone when that person has abused my body and forced me to do things I never intended to do? How can I make a friend when I don't trust anyone? How can I open up to another person after my ex cheated on me, or after I found out what my old friends said about me?

My mentor, Judy, has the answer for that.

"Just be," she says.

Once upon a time there was a beautiful girl who used to trust. And then she learned the hard way that not everyone could be trusted, especially the people she thought would never hurt her – like her father.

She went to school and heard all the kids talking about their families. "My daddy is amazing; my mommy is so sweet; my daddy bought me a phone; my mommy always hugs and kisses me and tells me how incredible I am."

The girl thinks: "Blah blah blah blah. BS. Not everyone is blessed with awesome parents."

This girl's father made her his sex toy. He told her to do things or she'd be living on the street.

She used to run around the playground the way kids do – laughing, playing games, and watching The Wiggles on TV. Then, all of a sudden it seemed, she developed an adult body, boobs, ass. And that's when all hell broke loose, when her dad started to look at her differently.

Now she doesn't know how to trust anyone. Not friends. Not a boyfriend. Especially not a boy. Every guy is just like her dad.

She thinks: Why am I the unlucky one? Fathers aren't supposed to make their daughters feel uncomfortable. They're supposed to protect their daughters from bad things.

How can she trust when she was abused? Trust simply isn't an option.

Of course, her experience is the extreme, and completely life-changing. She DOES have a big reason not to trust anybody, but maybe you do, too. Maybe your friends laughed at you as a kid and it made you think: People aren't to be trusted.

We can tell ourselves: "I choose to trust myself. And I choose to let go of my past. My past is not my present – it's only my story. It makes me stronger. I choose to trust. I choose to trust that not everyone is like the people who broke my trust."

We don't always have to figure things out. We don't always have to worry about what he will do or if he will try to kiss me on the first date. We should "just be", the way Judy says. We can ask ourselves, as Emily says, "How can I be more present today?"

Sometimes we can't trust that today will be a good day. And letting go of that control is where we struggle.

Embrace your intuition

When our feelings tell us to do something, we should always listen. No matter what, our intuition will always be right. Maybe you're supposed to go to the biggest party of the year and your feeling tells you not to. Listen to that. It's your inner spark telling you not to do something. This feeling is your protection.

What if you go against your feelings and attend the party? And what if some drunken guy slips drugs into your drink? You never know. Listen to that feeling that is protecting you.

Your inner spark can also reveal a good feeling. Let's say you've recorded an entire track of music, and your dream is to get produced by a record label. For whatever reason, you keep feeling: Bring the track out on your lunch date with Grandma today.

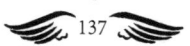

So you bring the CD with you. You get to the restaurant, you order your food, and guess who is sitting beside you? One of your favourite music producers. You take your chances and you give him your track. And you hope he will feel your passion, your energy.

Miracles do happen. They might happen in this case or they might not, but your inner feelings, listened to, have provided an opportunity. Miracles are all about trust. Do you trust that you will make your way safely through the winter snow into the calm and sunny summer? If you trust that, then maybe you will find your own miracles.
It's like what Emily said during our phone call: We need to trust that life will provide us with everything we deserve, need and want.

I choose to trust my inner spark.

Do you?

CHAPTER THIRTEEN
Love Yourself

TOOL 11: Love Yourself

Love makes us feel happy with ourselves.
It makes our world feel complete.

Love is something that we spend most of our lives trying to conquer. It's something we try to find in the people we meet, the relationships that form, the attractions we feel with another person, the approval of our parents or peers.

But when do we search for the love that is inside of us?

15 YEARS OLD

Yay. Today I'm seeing T'ameaux. I call her by the name I created: "Healer T". The name matches her purpose in my life, because she always seems to help me heal my problems.

She opens the door with a big smile.

"Welcome, beautiful one," she says.

We sit down in her healing room, which has many pillows, and crystal lamps. Calming music is playing in the background.

"How are you?" she asks.

I start to cry. For some reason, all my emotions have decided to come out in this exact moment.

I'm crying for all the times I look myself in the mirror and say: "I hate the way I look!"

I'm crying for the time the boy I liked didn't like me back, and I thought it was because I was ugly.

I'm crying because I don't feel attractive.

I'm crying because I don't love myself.

"Stand up Britt," Healer T says.

I stand up. And listen. Tears and black makeup still drip down my face.

"Look yourself in the mirror," she says. "Find your gaze. Look directly into your eyes. Look at your body. Look how beautiful you really are."

Well. That makes it worse. It makes me cry even more.

"I don't love anything about myself," I yell. "Look at those legs! Listen to how annoying my voice sounds! Look at my face! I look like a baby!"

"Stop that," Healer T says. "Those are your negative thoughts. You've grown up relying on these thoughts. Break it now. And let's start over. What do you LOVE about yourself?"

This is tricky. Because I hate everything about myself.

"I guess I love my hair," I hear myself saying. "I guess I love my blue eyes. I love my kind heart."

"Now," says Healer T, "say: I love myself."

I couldn't get the words out.

"I love…" I started. But I choked. I couldn't get the word "myself" out.

Finally, I did it.

"I love myself," I said. "I love myself. I love myself."

The warm, calming feeling that is going through me is something I never thought was possible to feel.

I'm beginning a new journey of loving myself. Today I'm taking the first step.

I do love myself. I am enough. My body. Mind. And soul. They're all good enough.

I am loved.

Ready to love yourself?

We all have times in our lives when we can't seem to say: "I love myself."

At times like that, it doesn't matter who tells you "You're beautiful", because you will never believe them.

If we don't love ourselves first, relationships won't last very long, because how can you expect somebody to love you when you don't even *like* yourself? You'll always think: Does he really think I'm beautiful? Does he really like me? Am I good enough for her?

When I didn't love myself fully, that meant I didn't love my mind, body or soul. I ate junk food that only made my body weaker. I instilled negative thoughts, which made my mind weaker. I didn't follow my heart's desire, which only made me fight what my soul really wanted.

You can do the same thing. You have a mind that needs to be taken care of. You have a body that needs to be healthy. You have a soul that needs love and nourishment.

Educate your mind

Falling down, getting back up. This is how we learn: from making mistakes.

I started reading last summer, when I discovered that writing is my biggest passion. I wanted to be a better writer, so I read, and read, and read. I keep reading to expand my mind, to learn and gain more knowledge.

Imagine putting yourself into a world a fiction writer has created for you. Read about something you're passionate about. Read self-help books and keep educating yourself on how to lead a happier life.

Expand your knowledge.

- Read the newest best seller
- Read the newspaper
- Watch inspirational movies
- Watch documentaries
- Travel, if you can
- Ask adults questions about their lives and what they learned so far. Perhaps visit a seniors' home.
- Go to the library (and *don't* say "boring")
- Talk to new people.

Tell me one thing you've done to educate yourself. Besides school.

LISTEN TO YOUR SOUL

What does your heart feel? What are you passionate about? What do you feel? This is about the feeling inside of you. This is about who you are. This is about liking your personality. Your soul is who you are.

YOU.

Going against what our soul or heart feels is something we do often: "Should I sleep with him or not? Should I be with her or not?"

This is a big topic. *Sex.*

My mentor Judy told me: "Always do what you feel is right in your heart, and listen to your body. It will determine whether or not you are ready to lose your virginity."

A lot of times we think to ourselves: "How do I know if I should do it or not?"

That's easy. Are you doing it because everybody in school has lost their virginity? Or are you doing it because your body is saying: "I'm ready to take this big step into womanhood [or manhood]?"

You'll just know.

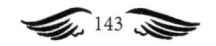

Afterwards you may regret it, not because "you weren't ready", but because maybe it wasn't the experience you wish it could have been. Or maybe it will be the best experience ever, and that is super okay. Listen to you heart. What is it saying? Listen to your soul. What is it desiring?

Don't regret anybody you sleep with. Are you wondering why? Because every person teaches us a lesson.

My friend messaged me: "I'm stupid. I slept with Blake. I regret it. I never wanted to. I think I did it because everybody is having sex in our generation and I don't want to be the only one who still remains a virgin."

BIG NO-NO. Why put yourself into that situation? You'll just be fighting what your soul really wants.

There are two fights we do with our heart and soul: First, our body wants to lose its virginity and have sex, but we fight it because we are scared of the outcome. Second, we aren't ready and we only do it because people at school are doing it.

Which fight is yours?

Sex Checklist.

Reflect on your first time. Acknowledge your fears. What does sex mean to you?

- ♡ It gave me pleasure or it was meant to give me pleasure
- ♡ It is meant for people who are madly in love.
- ♡ I felt pressured and forced.
- ♡ Everyone else is doing it, so why not me?
- ♡ Sex goes against my beliefs and morals.
- ♡ I usually regret it in the morning.
- ♡ I am scared it will hurt.
- ♡ Sex before marriage is wrong.
- ♡ It will make your partner love you.
- ♡ It will keep you and your partner together for a long time.
- ♡ I can only be drunk when I have sex.

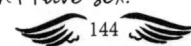

- ♡ I expect sex to be perfect.
- ♡ I expect sex to be with the person I love.
- ♡ My body is ugly and fat, which is why I can't have sex.
- ♡ I do it so my parents can find out.
- ♡ I don't want my parents to find out, so I never have sex.
- ♡ I am comfortable with my boyfriend; we laugh about everything.
- ♡ I don't think it is okay to be a virgin.
- ♡ I don't want anyone finding out.
- ♡ I can't wait for everyone to discover I am not a virgin.
- ♡ I am not comfortable with my body.
- ♡ My parents told me sex is for adults only.

NOURISH YOUR SOUL

We should live everyday doing something that fuels our soul with excitement.

This is what I like to do: maybe you'll find it helpful, too.

- Meditation.
- Music.
- Walk in nature.
- Inspiring movies, like documentaries.
- Reading meaningful books, and books that relate to our lives.
- Bath, lit candles, relaxing music (my favorite)
- Intellectual and deep conversations with like-minded people.

If you live every day feeding your soul with love, with what it wants, and don't fight it then you will be happy.

If you make your choices because your heart is calling for it, go ahead and do it. We fight our emotions. We fight our connections with others. We are always fighting something. And that is no way to love your soul.

Do you listen to your soul? If so, tell me what you do exactly to become in touch with your deepest feelings.

What nourishes your soul? Music? Dance? Yoga? Something that calms the lion. That's a saying... However, tell me one thing that calms you down after a busy day.

Love your body

Give your body foods that make you stronger, healthier, and happier.

I learned that our body deserves to be nourished, loved, and accepted. We need to be nourished with healthy foods. In the same way we should think positively, we should give ourselves "positive foods".

I know that's a lot to ask. Who doesn't want chocolate? Who doesn't want chips?

So we have to learn to eat them in small portions. Every day we can have a treat, but we have to remember that what we give our body, what we eat, is what we become.

What you eat, becomes your result.

Before I eat something really unhealthy, I say: "I trust that this food will give me the proper nutrition."

It's not about being skinny or fat, because a number never defines a person's beauty. It's about staying healthy, strong, and active.

Step one: Eat breakfast

Step two: Eat fruits and vegetables at least once a day

Step three: Move your body. Go on a walk. Or a jog. Go to yoga. Go to the gym. Go for a swim. There are so many ways to move our bodies. Take dance classes. Get outside, and let the sun shine on you, despite how much you like to stay home, watch television, or play video games. Get sleep. At least 7-8 hours a night.

Step four: Love everything about yourself.

Last year...

Chips after chips. Cookies after cookies. Cake after cake. Chocolate after chocolate.

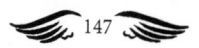

Those were my daily foods. I ate when I was sad. I ate when I was nervous. I ate when I was angry. I abused my body with foods that consumed my mind into thinking they would make me feel happier.

There are three things we can do to fully love ourselves: Love our body, give our body proper foods, and exercise.

If you're anything like me, going to the gym is AWFUL and BORING. I can't run on the treadmill. It's not my thing. But I can go on long hikes, or walks. *That* is my thing.

Yoga has been my daily practice to balance my mind, body and soul. It's a workout, it's a practice to stay calm, and it limits negative thinking. It's a win-win situation. In the next chapter, you'll have your own yoga class!

We can't just love one without the other two. It balances each other out. Mind. Soul. Body.

I hope your daily intentions will become: "I choose to love myself. I choose to balance my body, mind and soul."

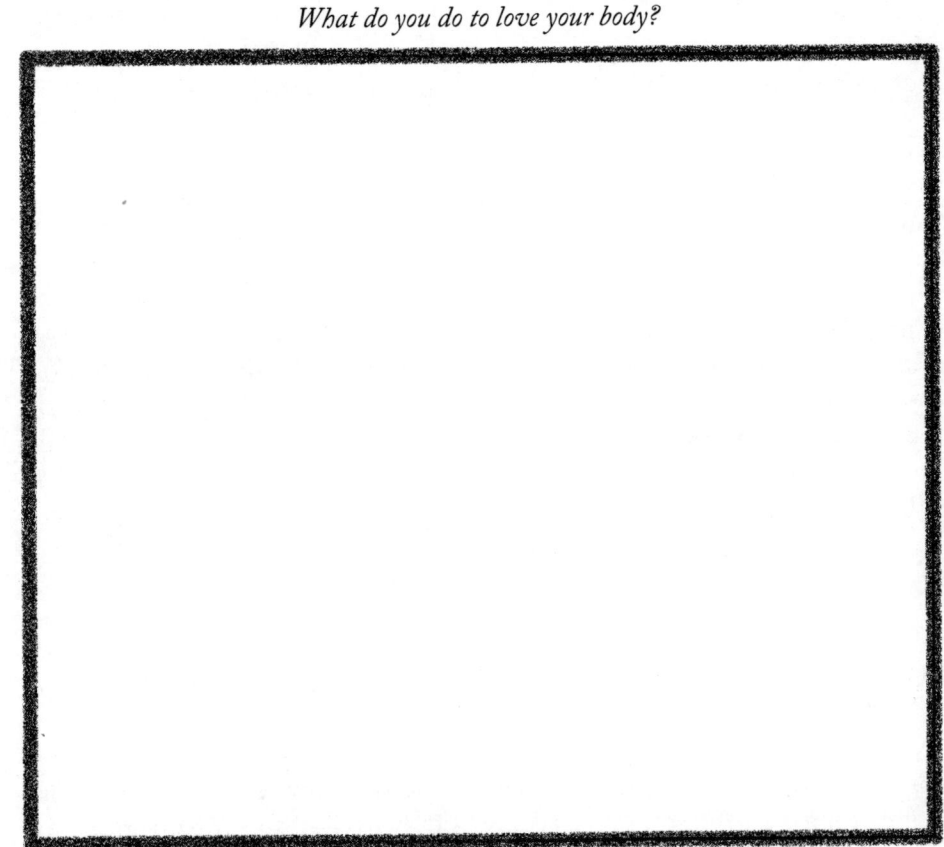

What do you do to love your body?

CHAPTER FOURTEEN
Yoga

Yoga is nothing more than stretches.
Yoga is OM.
Yoga is for Buddhists.
Yoga is easy.
Yoga is for hippies.

Wrong.

Yoga changed my life. It gave me the chance to look at myself in the mirror and say: I love myself.

Yoga. Just like that, one day turned into two days. Yoga turned into every day. It became my life, both on and off the mat.

You should try it.

My instructor, Paria, was there from the start, in my very first class. She saw me fall out of poses. She watched me get frustrated. She knew I was thinking: This isn't how I should look!

She also witnessed me transform into the person I am today: confident, brave, and happy.

This chapter brings you the magic of Paria's class.

"My greatest joy is to watch my students grow to their fullest potential," she told me. I want to share her story and help her to help you to grow into your body, mind and soul.

Get ready. This is your journey. You are not alone. Paria is your teacher. Lean on her words. Let her yoga sequence give you hope.

Introducing: the awesome and beautiful Paria Mirazimi.

Yoga is the Dance of My Life
By Paria Mirazimi

I used to do competitive dance. I got lost in dance. It was me and the music: nothing else mattered. It took away my anxiety.

I quit dance in Grade 10. I was caught up in school… and perfection. I thought I needed perfect marks. Perfect hair. Perfect body. Perfect personality. High marks.

Perfection was high-stress and it consumed my entire life. I needed another outlet.

I went online and searched Yoga studios in Toronto. The first one that came up was "Moksha Yoga, Richmond Hill". What's Moksha? I wondered. Was it a type of yoga? Was it a studio? Would I like it?

My mom drove me there. I took the introductory offer. And I can remember the first class. I was hooked.

It was an instant connection. It was a chance to move my body, to breathe my stress out and to be myself.

Later, when I was training to be a yoga teacher, I knew I wanted to be able to heal people. If I could touch at least one person's heart, then I would know I had accomplished my purpose.

Now Yoga is my dance. And dance is my life.

You can do this, too. Yoga isn't "weird". Yoga can change your life, if you let it.

Take it seriously. Once my friend, Carmelinda and I were teaching at a high school. Carm taught a class in the theatre and I taught in the gym. Kids were giggling. They were mocking yoga. The coolest girl was trying to impress the coolest boy. They both went into the practice with no intention of taking it seriously.

After 10 minutes, I noticed they were smiling. They were also becoming more serious. I thought: They're enjoying this!

Practice at home – in your bedroom, your living room or anywhere you can find empty space. Establish a routine. Do this when you wake

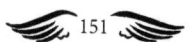

up or before you go to sleep. Tell yourself: I will let go. I will not hold onto any expectations.

Start with: Meditation

Sit comfortably and close your eyes. Start to connect to your breathing. Follow your inhales and exhales. Don't try to control your breathing. Just absorb the way the air flows throughout your body. Then catch your breath. Take this moment to be perfectly still and to let your thoughts go. Nothing else should matter. It's just you and your breath.

Inhale. Take three slow, full, breaths. Notice how you feel when the breath enters your body. Inhale and say this mantra: "I send myself love".

Exhale. Release the air for four slow full breaths. Notice how you feel when you breathe the air out. Exhale and say: "I send love to someone who needs it."

Meditation never has a time limit. It could just be for three minutes, or five, or an hour. It's up to you. Just make sure you do a full set:

Inhale for three counts.

Exhale for four counts.

Yoga for YOU

Half Salutations
Do this three to five times.

Mountain Pose

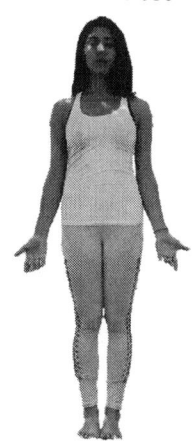

Prayer Pose

First: Inhale with your arms over your head. Touch your palms.

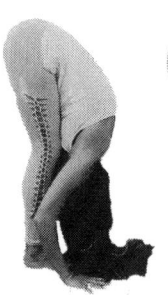

Second: Exhale Fold all the way forward. Hands go on your mat.

Third: Inhale half way, heart opens, chest rises. Place your hands on your shins and lengthen your spine.

Then, Exhale. Return your hands back to your mat. You can bend your knees if you can't touch your mat fully. Press through your feet. Inhale and circle your arms up overhead. Touch your palms.

Fourth: Exhale, bring your palms to your heart center.

Once you're finished, close your eyes again. Bring your hands to your heart. Set an intention (i.e., I am going to live more in the present.)

Standing back bend:

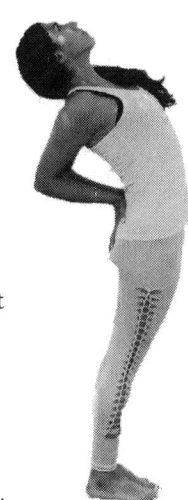

Put your palms on your sacrum (the flat triangular-shaped bone located at the base of your spine).

- Bring your elbows closer together behind your back.
- Inhale. Lift your chest. Your heart will open. (This could be where you connect to what your heart really wants)
- Return to Mountain Pose. Stay here for three full sets of breaths (In for three, out for four). Connect to your intention. What is it you're lacking in your life? What is it you want to feel?
- Take one big inhaled breath with your arms overhead. Put your palms together.
- Exhale and fold forward. Bring your hands to your mat. If you can't touch the mat, you can bend your knees a bit.

High Lunge:

- Do this with three sets of breaths.
- Inhale and bring your hands to your shins.
- Exhale and bring your hands to the mat.
- Bend your knees. Step your left leg back into a lunge.
- Inhale with your arms all the way up to the ceiling.
- Exhale and do a gentle backbend.

Repeat on the other side:
- Exhale and bring your hands to the floor.
- Bend your left knee.
- Step forward.
- Bring your hands to your shins. Keep a flat back.
- Exhale and bring your hands down. Step your right leg back to a lunge.
- Inhale with your arms all the way up to the ceiling.
- Exhale and do a gentle backbend.

Out of that pose:
Put your hands on the floor. Step your right foot forward. Put your hands on your shins, with a flat back. Exhale and fold. Bring your hands down to the mat.

Inhale. Circle your arms over your head.

Exhale and bring your hands to your heart.

Pause.

Take a full breath in:
1-inhale,
2-inhale,
3-inhale.

Exhale and bring your arms to your sides.

This is another chance where you could connect back to your intention. What is it you want to experience or feel?

Warrior 1:

- Take three full sets of breaths throughout the pose: 1-2-3. Exhale. 1-2-3-4
- Bring your hands to your hips.
- Step your left leg back (about four inches behind you)
- Turn your left foot on a 45-degree angle.
- Square your hips forward.
- Bend to your right knee.
- Inhale with your arms up overhead.

Repeat on other side

Most people hate this pose, but you'll learn to love it. Step into your power!

Warrior 2:

- Take three sets of breaths.
- Exhale with your arms parallel to the ground.
- Heel-toe and bring your left leg back.
  The outer edge of your left leg should be parallel to the mat.
- Gaze forward to your right middle finger.
- Heel to arch: intersect the right heel at the left heel.

Out of that pose:
Bend your right knee and come to standing pose.

Repeat on the other side:
Heel-toe and bring your right leg back.
Bend your left knee.
Gaze forward to your left middle finger.

Out of that pose:
Put your hands on your hips.
Straighten your right leg.
Heel-toe, left foot in.
Step to the front of the mat.

Mountain pose:
- Inhale with your arms overhead. Touch your palms together.
- Exhale and fold forward.
- Inhale and place your hands on your shins.
- Exhale and bring your hands to the ground.
- Hands should be shoulder width.
- Step your right foot back.

Now you're in High Plank:

- Take three sets of breaths.
- Inhale and engage your belly. (Inhale 1.2.3. and Exhale perfectly, too.

Downward dog:

- Take three sets of breaths.
- Exhale and press your hips upwards.
- If you're feeling tight, try pedaling through your heels by bending one knee at a time.

Child pose:

Hold this pose for as long as you want. This is your quiet time.
- Drop your knees to the ground.
- Bring your toes together.
- Sit your bum on your heels.
- Stretch your arms forward.
- Bring your forehead down to the mat.

Ask yourself: How do I feel? This is a time to reconnect. And it's another moment to come back to your intention.

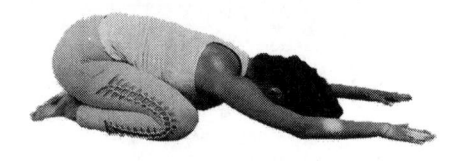

I was the "over achiever" in high school. I always needed to be perfect. I struggled with fears that everything I did wasn't good enough.

If you're that teen, always trying to go above and beyond, I hope this yoga will help you to let go of your own harsh judgments of yourself.

Remember: You don't have to be anything but yourself.

I often get asked: Why do you love teaching yoga?

"I love the way I get to hold a space for others," I answer. "It's a chance to go on a journey with my students, because my students are actually my teachers.
What if I'm in a bad mood that day?

My students are my number-one priority. I need to let go of my own shit in order to serve them.

The coolest part about teaching is that every person who walks into the room is different. It doesn't matter who it is. Everyone is coming to the mat for a purpose.

Some come to lose weight. Some come to help with their depression. Some come to get away from a busy world. Others use the space to relax their minds, to have quiet time.

We all come to this place to heal. I love crowded classes. Sometimes there are more than 50 people. Mats are literally on top of each other. Some teachers dislike it, but I love it. Why? Because I get the chance to hold a space for a large community to support each other. Note the little word "unity" in that bigger word, community.

The more people the better!
When people come to yoga for a physical workout, I like to watch it becoming more than a workout for them. I get to see doors open. These are the moments I always cherish. People sometimes come into the studio insecure, angry, upset and negative. But soon I see them transforming – becoming brave and confident and happy.

This is a long journey. I love seeing the transformation. I hope this helps you find your path.

We are connected through each movement, each breath and each time you do the sequence I have outlined on these pages.

I'm happy I took the time to find an outlet I could get lost in. I found it. It's yoga, the dance of my life.

The light within me bows, honors and acknowledges the light within you. Always let it shine.

From my heart to yours,

Namaste.

Paria Mirazimi

CHAPTER FIFTEEN
Divine Timing

"Everything happens for a reason"

is what my mentor, Healer T told me.

This is what I've learned: when hard times strike, I instantly feel caught off guard, all I want is answers. Does this ever happen to you?

You ask questions like, "Why is this happening to me of all people? G-d what did I do wrong? Why didn't Josh like me back. Why did my neighbor torment me? Why don't I have any friends? Why is my health so bad? Why are people gossiping about me?"

I told you in the beginning of the book that you, "Will get through all life's challenges" I was right, wasn't I? Life is holding you. Life is always giving you an invitation to keep fighting. You are a warrior. A fighter. You're still alive, still breathing, than you've become one of the strongest people ever!

I was at the bookstore today and I wanted to find this particular book. There was only one left in the bookstore. I couldn't' find it. I kept thinking, "Where the heck could it be?"

I thought, 'under the shelves', nope. What about above the shelves? Nope. I almost gave up."

Until I walked into the cook food section, and it was on the floor, the last book in the store. See how there is a force so much larger than us, bringing us to the right places, showing us the things we've only dreamed of. Only if 'it's meant to be', it'll happen.

People call this 'divine timing', or perfect timing. Meeting the right people unexpectedly, and we say: "It's so meant to be!"

Someone once said to me: "It might not feel this way right now, but just as the oak tree, folded and invisible, lies who within the acorn, so everything you need to live through this current mess of life is within you."

You're beautiful ~ strong ~ brave ~ blessed ~ You have arrived in this chapter at the perfect time.

You have everything you need to make it through this difficult world.

Remember, if this crisis wasn't meant to be in your life, than it never would have happened in the first place. Everything we do, meet and see in this lifetime happens for a reason. Sucks at times, right? Amazing at times, right?

Come on, you're here, your journey is never ending. Pause. Take a break. Breathe. I'll pass this saying my mentor always reminds me: "You've arrived."

Do you believe everything happens for a reason? If so, tell me a time something happened that you gasped: wow thank god this happened.

CHAPTER SIXTEEN

Her Evil Reflection

There's the story of the girl who doesn't like the image that reflects back at her.

This could relate to every teen girl who doesn't like her body image. The negative influences on television tell her: "You're so fat! Go lose some pounds, Loser!"

It's not fair.

"You're stupid" are two words that have the ability to break a person's soul.

Today sucks.

I called my mom to pick me up because Maya called me fat, ugly, stupid, loser.

I will not cry. I will not let her win. I will not show her my weakness. I won't break because of her mean words. I'm better than this.

So I call my mom.

"I don't feel good," I say. "Please pick me up?"

My mom drops me off at home. I run to my bedroom, pick up the pillows and throw them. I throw all the picture frames my mom has placed on my dresser. I throw my phone. I push all the clothes that are hanging neatly in the closet.

Mom won't be too happy over this mess.

But who cares?

I'm sick of feeling powerless. I'm sick and tired of letting people control me, and letting their words affect me.

Am I really ugly? Am I really fat? Am I really not good enough? Am I really a loser? Am I really not cool enough?

I squeeze my eyes shut and bury my head into the palms of my hand.

I bend over and collapse on the floor. I am crying. And crying. And crying. I can taste the salty tears dripping down my face.

I have tried before to fight this emotion, to refuse to allow people to get to me. But I'm too late. They already have.

My hands start to shake. My body weakens.

"When will I be good enough?" I yell.

I regain a bit of strength. I pull myself up from the messy floor. I throw my necklace that says "You're beautiful, inside and out" at the reflection in the mirror of a girl I no longer know.

I used to be happy. I didn't care what others thought of me. I used to do whatever I wanted. People could laugh or roll their eyes or gossip about me, and I didn't care.

Things have changed. Now I watch the pathetic loser in the mirror, sobbing like a crazy girl.

I hate every minute that goes by. I see weakness in the reflection in the way that girl is holding herself up. I see fear in her eyes. I see pain.

She is my worst enemy. We move towards each other. We hold our fist up and smash it. Tiny pieces fall all over me and onto the floor. It feels as though each little piece is a symbol of my evil perception of myself.

Each piece defines the hatred I feel for myself, and the feeling I get when people laugh at me. It defines the feeling I get when I don't like the way I look in a bathing suit, or when I get out of the shower and avoid looking at myself in the mirror.

I look up and there is no longer a reflection staring back at me. It has been my own enemy, an enemy inside my mind. The enemy has listened to the mean comments and laughed at my appearance.

My tears stop. I look around me and notice what I did in the midst of my impulsive emotions. Silently, I laugh a little.

What if I loved my reflection? I ask myself. Would I blossom like a butterfly and shine like the sun, with joy, happiness, and confidence?

That's my dream – to love my reflection.

Yoga instructors say: Use your yoga off the mat.

When you close this book, I hope you will use the tools and inspiration you may have felt. I hope this reading journey will continue after you've read each page.

Here are a few pointers to bring you a smile whenever you feel defeated in this hectic world.

- ♡ Let your voice shine. Choose to speak your truth.
- ♡ Only "chill" or hangout with positive people. Choose to surround yourself with people who uplift you and accept you for who you really are.
- ♡ Chase that nervous feeling. Choose to step out of your comfort zone.
- ♡ Don't hold onto things for comfort. Choose to let things come and go like a river, without holding on to any attachments.
- ♡ Never underestimate your worth. Choose to remind yourself of your worth when you feel sad.
- ♡ You always belong somewhere. Choose to remind yourself that being different is okay. Wherever you go, you belong. This is your home.
- ♡ Be empathetic. Choose to understand people before judging them.
- ♡ Never feel discouraged by your mistakes. Choose to learn from all your mistakes and bad choices.
- ♡ Be nice and have respect for others. Choose to live with your heart, helping those in need whenever you can.

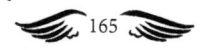

♡ Trust. Choose to trust yourself most of all.

♡ Don't take things personally. Choose to remind yourself that other people have bad days, too.

♡ Don't think you're better than anyone else. Choose to live with the knowledge that nobody is better. We are all one.

♡ Express your true self without worrying about what anyone thinks. Choose to be yourself, no matter who is watching, judging, or criticizing. You are you. Beautiful. Strong. Loveable.

♡ Love yourself. Choose to love yourself no matter what your reflection or your mind tell you.

A CONVERSATION WITH SEVEN YEAR OLD ME

I'm speaking on the phone to Emily, one of my mentors.

"In order to heal our past," she says, "we need to accept and nourish our younger selves. Try it, Britt."

She continues: "Talk to your seven-year-old self," she says. "Close your eyes. Visualize your old house. Can you see your room? Envision yourself – as you are now – speaking to her. Talk to the little girl who is hurt and weak, the little girl who cries silently all alone in her room, the little girl who is wishing and hoping for a way out of the pain."

I clear my mind from distractions and do what she suggests.

This should be easy, I tell myself. Or not.

I see myself as I am now: strong, brave. Wearing my jeans and tank top. I walk up to my old house. I take a big breath. I am strong. I can face the old me.

HER EVIL REFLECTION

I walk to the front door. My heart is beating fast. I see 7-year-old Britt in the living room. She's wearing a sundress. Her hair is past her shoulders. Her bangs cover her forehead.

I hear a voice in the background: "Go away, Brittany. Leave my friends and me alone. Nobody wants you here. Go to your room! And stay there!" It's big sister.

Tears are falling down her face. She walks upstairs with her shoulders down. Her world has crashed. She opens her pink room and looks at all the dolls. She hugs one.

"Nobody loves me," she says.

Now she's sitting on the floor with her arms folded over her knees. Seeing her so weak, so restless, breaks my heart. I want to heal her. Take her pain away. Tell her how amazing she really is.

I walk through the door of her room. She looks at me. There's fear in her eyes.

"I'm not going to hurt you," I say. "I promise."

I lower myself to the ground. I'm unable to take my eyes off this beautiful, sad, angelic and fragile little girl.

She lifts her head off her knees and looks at me again.

She looks lifeless. I feel tears welling in my eyes. She needs me to be strong for her. There's no happiness in her eyes.

I reach my hand out to her. I look down and see the hand of the younger me, my child's hand. I'm holding onto the hand of the future.

"Britt," I say. "Do you know how brave you are?" She just shakes her head.

I continue: "You might think nobody loves you, because you can't find the confidence to speak for yourself yet. You sit in the corner of the classroom, avoiding people, living in a separate world. It doesn't feel good when your sister won't allow you to hang out with her friends, does it? It makes you ask what's wrong with you.

"Why are you brave? Because you're getting through each day without speaking to anyone. You're handling it all on your own."

Brittany wraps her arms around my neck and buries her head into my chest. She cries.

"You're going to be okay," I say.

"How do you know that?" she asks.
"Because I've lived this life," I answer. "And look at me now. I made it!"

I say more.

"One day you're going to speak for the first time," I begin. "There will be a day when you get laughed at in class. That will make you feel awful. But you'll get through it. People might call you names. They'll say 'Brittany is a loser. She's weird.' That will hurt.

"You'll go home, lock yourself in your room, and wonder why you're still fighting this life.

"You'll make it through, though. Why? Because you're one of the bravest souls on this earth."

I continue to hold her and to wipe her tears with my thumb.

"Just because people at school don't 'get' you," I say, "it doesn't mean you're any less than anyone else. Just because your family doesn't understand you doesn't make you worthless. Please remember that. When life gets hard, please remember how brave, beautiful and strong you are."

She's trembling against my chest. She's letting someone love her. She's letting someone take care of her, letting someone inside her mind.

"I wish I had you to protect me from all the bad things people say behind my back," she says, "or all the times I'm not allowed to hang out with Sissy. Or all the times I'm afraid to speak."

These words break my heart. This poor little girl is feeling all alone in the world.

"I'm always here," I tell her. "I'm inside your heart, mind and soul. Look at me as the 'higher' you: the one who has gone through many more years of experience. I have gained strength. I'm your strength. I'm your courage. I'm your bravery.

"Every time you speak up for the kid who gets bullied, that's me. Every time you speak up when your daddy or mommy yell at you, that's me. Every time you take courage to share your story with the world, that's me. Never forget that. Promise me?"
"I promise," she says.

"One more thing. I promise I won't let you go. I won't forget you. I'm going to hold you, the younger me, and carry you around in my heart forever. Eventually, all the bad memories won't be remembered as a bad thing – but only as memories of the little girl who was strong."

All of a sudden we hear giggles coming from Sissy and her friends. We hold onto each other more tightly. We're making sure we both know we're not alone.

"I love you, Brittany," I say. "You're going to rock it. You're going to save the world. Your voice is your weapon."

And then, to myself, I amend that. WE are going to rock it.

CHAPTER SEVENTEEN
I See You

I've always believed everything I do becomes a chapter in my life story – all the heartbreaks, all the days where I can't manage to get out of bed, all the crying, all the struggling. It has all become my life story.

Just like everybody else in this world – they have or have had a struggle that isn't spoken about. And isn't acknowledged. But... it's their life story.

Your story

The past becomes a chapter in our book, and the future will be added later on. So, if you think about it like that, we are just like a book.

I'm a big believer in sharing all our chapters. And saying: "I went through this. It was crappy. It sucked. I cried. I yelled. It was the worst time in my life" (of course with more details) – but also: "I got through it."

We got through it!

What you went through might save the person who is going through that same struggle right now. It's the only way we can change the world. We can come together and show each other we are never really alone.

Thank you to everybody who shared a story. It takes a lot of bravery to share something so personal with the world. And even if you left your name anonymous, it still takes a lot of courage to put yourself out there. I thank you from the bottom of my heart. Your story is touching lives right now.

This chapter is for the teen who wants to feel understood. This is for the teen who wants somebody to look at him or her and say: **"I see your potential. I understand your feelings. I notice your strength. I see you. You're never alone."**

Have you ever felt alone? Have you ever felt like nobody is watching you? Has there been a time you were misunderstood?

Well you are not.

```
            I see you.
```

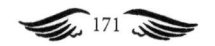

Revi Riabinski

"I have learned something vital in the worst of situations. I wish I learned this much quicker, as opposed to waiting 16 long years.

This is something you have probably heard before, but might not have allowed yourself to accept. I cannot simply tell you this in one sentence, but I will try my best to elaborate what I am trying to convey.

When I was going through problems, I would just sit and wish for a miracle to occur. This only dragged out the problem and allowed it to last longer than it should.

Probably everybody feels stress before a test. I have stopped stressing out completely, because of this simple method.

I tell myself, what is the point of stressing so much if it will be over in an hour? This does not only work for tests, but for everything you might be stressed or worried about.

Another example is the uneasy feeling I get before the first day of school. I ask myself, what is the point of stressing about the first day of school when it will be over in a day? Why build all those negative thoughts preparing yourself for the first day of school when it will eventually end? This applies to everything in life. The more unhappy you are, the more problems you allow yourself to create – problems such as depression, suicidal thoughts and abuse.

Throughout my 16 years, I have realized I need to open my eyes and see that the problems I am facing now will be eventually be gone. Simply the act of being patient will move my life forward in a positive way."

Ashley Pereira

"My name is Ashley-Ann. I'm 21 years old. I currently work full-time in the social services field and part-time building a business for young people to help them discover their direction and passions. I want to give young people the resources for success and to support them along their journey.

I am a motivational speaker. When I was growing up, I was the girl who had no confidence and no love for myself. Something happened. I surrounded myself with new people who were positive and helped inspire me to emerge in the personal development world. I feel strongly about youth and female empowerment and traveling the world to volunteer in different countries.

I say this humbly because it has not always been this way for me. I went on a journey to find who I was – what I valued and what made me happy. When this became clear I discovered my purpose: my purpose is to serve. Once I discovered this, my confidence began to shine.

Know thyself is a saying I live by because I feel like this helped me build my confidence. It helped me love myself for who I am, when I didn't know who I was. My mission is to spread this exact message: knowing yourself creates possibilities that are endless."

Andrew Kaspiris

"When I was growing up, I never felt that I was a part of the 'social narrative'. I always felt out of place and that I didn't belong, so because of that I got into drugs and started hanging out with the wrong crowd in my attempt to fit into a group.

I realized that everyone is unique and that you need to embrace your imperfections and flaws because they are what make you YOU!"

Jenna

"Hi! My name is Jenna. I'm 14 years old and I have Lupus. Lupus is a chronic, autoimmune disease. It attacks your skin, bones, muscles, and your organs. I got diagnosed when I was 11 years old. It was really hard knowing that because I have a disorder I'm not like everyone else anymore. It was really hard just to go about my day and do what the other kids were doing. It bothered me so much and I always felt depressed.

But, after a while I just didn't care anymore. I'm a very stubborn teen. After two and a half years of having this disability, I learned to cope with it and push myself so I can get through the whole day. (Like I said before, I'm very stubborn.) Being stubborn has a good side and a bad side. The good side is that being stubborn makes me feel stronger because if I'm not being stubborn then I would probably go to the middle school's nurse's office every day and take pills. Heck, I would probably just stay home and do homeschooling. But I don't want that. The bad side of being stubborn is that even though it's good for me to push myself a little, at the end of the day I feel horrible. My muscles ache, I have a bad headache and all I want to do is either take a long hot shower or just fall asleep.

Even though I have these problems, I still have my spirit. People who truly know me would say that I'm funny, sarcastic, sweet, and a lot of other good things. Having Lupus made me more mature and made my eyes more open."

T M

"I was always the so called perfect girl. I was smart, I had so many friends and I also had the so-called perfect body. I loved everything about myself. I had no idea that would all change within a few months. They say high school is the best four years of your life. Well, that's not the case for me. I moved from a different school. I didn't know anyone so I had to start off with a fresh new slate, which I guess was okay, but I had no idea what I was walking into.

I became friends with these girls I thought were a perfect match, but they weren't. A couple weeks into being friends they started telling me that I was chubby, I wasn't skinny enough, that people should be able to see the outlines of my ribs. I started questioning myself and my body. Every night before bed I'd stare at my body through a mirror and I started pinching my skin to see where I could lose a few pounds. But I didn't do anything.

For the next few weeks the girls would just call me ugly, a cow and so on. I really started to hate my body. I decided to make a change whether it was healthy or not. I stopped eating breakfast and lunch. I would only eat dinner so my parents wouldn't notice anything. I did that for a few weeks and everyone, including me, could was seeing a difference. I was getting compliments, like: 'Wow, you look amazing.' Or: 'You have gotten so thin.'

I loved that! I loved how it was working but I still didn't think it was enough. Long story short, I started purging every night in the shower non stop. I had no idea I wasn't going to be able to control it. Eventually I became anorexic and so sick; but I loved my body and so did my friends. My purging became my everything, I couldn't and wouldn't stop until I was put into hospital, and that half a year in hospital is what saved my life. When I look back, I think to myself how dumb I was. How could I have been so stupid, how could I have let a couple of people I barely know break me and remake me?

I choose to share this story because I think growing up in our generation is a huge deal. I want everyone to know that everyone struggles with mental illness whether we want to admit it or not.

Never question your body. You are beautiful just the way you are and if you ever think about starving yourself, or purging please reach out. We are all human."

Judy Machado-Duque

"When I was growing up, I cried about going to school from kindergarten to end of grade 6! YES! I cried most days of the week and ESPECIALLY on Sundays! I would wake up Sunday morning so sad with that sick feeling in my stomach because school would start again the next day. My grades were not good. I was an introvert. I was so afraid to get into trouble with the teachers, and all I wanted was to be home-schooled by mom. I had some teachers who didn't help. They were mean and would scream at me all the time for not knowing the answer, or for not speaking up. As I grew up, I became more confident about who I am. I started to smile a lot more.

Although I didn't go to University or College after high school, I became obsessed with personal development (Google it). I couldn't stop reading or listening to anyone in that field. I became empowered and I attracted some positive friends into my life who supported me and loved me no matter what. I realized that life is all about what we can do for others, and when we begin to help others, our problems seem to go away so quickly."

Noreen Kassam

"I remember when I was twelve years old and being encouraged to change my outfit several times before leaving the house in order to avoid the premature cleavage that so distinctly protruded from my chest. It was like there was something obscenely wrong with my body. I was encouraged by my mother to make extreme efforts to pretend as though these lumpy clumps of fat were non-existent beneath my garments. The shame began right then.

Before I knew it, shopping for clothes started to feel like a walk through hell – because nothing quite fit me the way it fit on the less-endowed females in my class. Buttons would explode with sudden movements, and picking up a dropped pencil off the floor in grade eight never came without an extended stare from the boys' corner of the room.

The girly girls in my community preferred nail polish and earrings. They wore dresses that exposed their less-apparent curves and would hit up La Senza for fun to find the most padded of bras. Me? I chose to become a tom boy. I figured surrounding myself with soccer-playing boys, and Nintendo gatherings in the baggiest of clothes would prevent me from having to face the reality of this voluptuous and inappropriate body.

It wasn't until my late 20s that I came to the realization that I hadn't done anything wrong. In fact, I began to appreciate my double, sometimes triple Ds. Rather than hide the obvious, I'd celebrate the obvious! My self-esteem began to grow as I released the shame, and began to giggle over the fact that all these years I had been utterly ashamed of my God-given assets. I believed that men liked me for all the wrong reasons, and that love would never be possible because my personality would always be overthrown by the ever popular "rack" I was known for.

This all became clear after I hit rock bottom in my self-image talk. I deepened the wounds by entering into the fitness industry as a personal trainer – only to be showcased in large commercial gyms as the trainer with the largest breasts. Members were all physically oriented – and both the women and men would pay special attention to my curves. Our uniforms didn't help the situation either.

There came a point where I could cry if someone dared to photograph me. Any type of video would cause anxiety to the point where my arm pits, knee pits and elbow pits would heat up and I would convulse. It got so bad at one point that I avoided all social events completely. Clothes made me look terrible in the eyes of others. Hitting rock bottom meant nearing suicide.

It was in the depths of such darkness that I was able to overcome all this shame and self-hate. I realized that it was time to start loving my body, no matter how it looked. I realized that it wasn't others who were the problem – it was me! My own insecurities were creating more and more outside attention!

It makes sense when you understand that what you focus on grows. I attracted many inappropriate comments by my own paranoia. My true breakthrough came when I was asked to write down several things that I liked about my body each day. It wasn't long till I started to truly adore my body – and celebrate these curves. Sometimes I shower at the gym just for the sake of testing myself to see if I have what it takes to just be happy being me!

I encourage you to write everyday, three or four things that you truly love about yourself. What imperfections make you perfect? Remember you are beautiful and complete just the way you were delivered to earth!"

Jeanette

"This is a poem I wrote when I was a teen going through my struggles."
"Vocabulary, Grammar, Words, Description, Expression, Dialogue, Language, Communication, Voice.
They all fail me.
Tools used to bridge the gap between self and the outside world, and they all fail me.
What is one to do when the pangs of thought cannot be caught?
When dreams of the future cannot be sought?
Fears unable to be brought to light?
When actions and endeavours are out of sight;
AND THEREFORE OUT OF MIND...
Unable to grasp them so they slip away.
Imagine not knowing what to do or what to say to soothe the vicious cries,
To bring acknowledgment to the puzzled eyes,
And comfort to the troubled sighs.
I m a g i n e
Simply being unable to put a name to the demons inside,
A face to the voices that lie within.
Ignorant to the weapons one possesses to thwart the leaches that
Suck & Steal &Tear & Gnaw
At your happiness.
Oblivious to the fact that you aid the furies,
To make you their prey,
You analyze, and strategize on the negativity,
Unknowing you're descending on your own sanity...
Swoop
The claws dig in,
The sweet taste of sin,
The hunted becomes the hunter,
And back again.
But it's too late to clip its wings,
Just let it win."

Anonymous

"It started when I was 14. It took a few people to tell me. I was a good dancer, really talented but they said that I needed to lose weight. From then on I thought I would need to be skinny to be a good dancer. I was eating still but not that much. The pounds were just not budging. By the 11th grade I was puking up my dinner, I didn't tell anyone and kept everything to myself because I've always been closed up.

I had marks and scars on my thighs and on my hips which were hard to cover because dance clothes are revealing. By January I was eating either fewer than 500 calories per day or nothing at all. I wrote down very calorie I ate and burned, but I still didn't tell anyone. My friends were telling me I was so skinny, but I didn't see it, I didn't see it at all. I just saw the pudgy thighs and arms.

The summer of that year I was my lowest weight, which was 86lbs. I had dropped 37lbs in 6 months … I was so proud. I was also angry, moody, shaking and crying most of the time. That's when my anxiety started and I got obsessed with control. I trained until my feet were bleeding and my arms ached. I didn't even know why I was dancing anymore. I wasn't happy.

My turning point was in August when I tried on my competition dress to see if it still fit because I dropped a few more pounds during training camp. I only took up half of the dress. I couldn't compete in it so we had to rent another one. What also helped me was becoming vegan and learning to eat healthy. It has been almost 2 years since then, and I'm still fighting every day. It's rare that I like what I see in the mirror, but at least I recognize it and at least I'm trying. I've never felt more comfortable in my body than I do now, I hope that I will soon be able to never relapse again and love myself once and for all. What is it worth, hating yourself all the damn time? Just live, and breathe and enjoy what life has given you day by day. That's the best you can do."

Emily Albert: *Internal Lightness*

"I was diagnosed with Anorexia Nervosa two years ago.

It's an eating disorder that had me admitted to hospitals where I wasted away my teen years for over a year in total: two four-month in-patient admissions at BC Children's Hospitals Eating Disorders Inpatient Unit, and two three-month admissions at Victoria General Hospital's Pediatric Cardiac Unit.

Over the past two torturous years of my life, I have learned to understand the true meaning to a saying I have been hearing for my entire life: 'Live life to the fullest'.

It started off as just wanting to be healthy and a way to bring myself to the top of my game. Back then I was training program for professional ballet. I was well on my way to achieving the life I had been dreaming of. Every time I looked into a mirror I seemed only to be able to focus on the little rounding of my stomach, so this led me to the conclusion that 'losing a few' could only improve my dancing. My exact thought was 'well, come on, if I lose some weight, then the roundness of my stomach will be gone. I will be able to concentrate on my dancing not my stomach during class. Right?'

After losing those five pounds, I learned my answer, and man was I ever wrong!! Losing those five pounds only made it worse! I started to notice my legs, my arms, and every single extra piece of skin, fat, and bulge that was completely unnecessary to me at the time. I now realize that I probably didn't have extra anything on me. I was ninety-seven pounds. I have always been a naturally skinny person, but all I saw was a person who was in dire need of losing weight.

I think I was at about ninety-two pounds when my dance teacher decided to say something. She had decided that I needed to gain weight. The head of the school told me that in one week I needed to gain three pounds, and if I didn't gain the weight, I was not allowed to dance anymore. With extreme difficulty, I added an apple a day onto the calories I had planned for myself, which definitely was not enough to gain, let alone even maintain my weight.

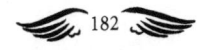

A week went by and sure enough, I had lost about five more pounds. What I heard come out of my teachers mouth ripped my heart out of my chest. It almost killed me. She told me that I was not able to live *my dream any longer. I was no longer allowed to do the one thing that mattered to me.*

I could no longer dance.

In that moment I felt no need and no purpose to live any longer.

The next thought to cross my mind was: 'Holy shit! I'm not dancing anymore. That means I'm not burning calories! That means I am going to gain weight!'

I had to take matters into my own hands; I needed to cut my calories down drastically and exercise 24/7. I would stay up all night doing sit-ups, push-ups, jumping jacks, and many other exercises. Every moment, and every second of my life was consumed by the monster living inside my head. I whittled myself down to 80-pound , five-foot-five girl who was covered in lanugo (fine white hairs all over my body) and I was always freezing cold. I was killing myself.

I started to take notice of intense pains in my chest , an unfathomable, cringe-worthy pain in my back, and the fact that when I stood up I would get so dizzy that I would stumble over to a wall and fall into it. I would start to shake, I was having seizures because of fluid and sodium loss. I knew something was going on but wasn't sure what. I was still in complete denial about having anorexia, despite what the counselors, doctors, therapists, psychiatrists, and family told me. All I knew was that I needed to lose weight.

I finally went ahead and told my parents about the pain in my back, thinking this was okay to tell them. I thought they wouldn't think too much about it because kidney disease runs in our family. However, my parents knew my pain was a result of my eating disorder attacking away my organs, since that was all my body had left to eat.

What happened next I could not prepare myself for. My parents dragged me to the hospital kicking, screaming, and punching in all possible directions. Scratch marks covered my face from my complete and utter frustration. (Which I have to admit didn't help my case in the slightest when I first arrived at the hospital.)

You can never predict how you are going to react to receiving news from a hoard of doctors: 'Emily, your tests have come back. Your kidneys and heart shutting down. Your brain is deteriorating. If you do not change what you are doing to yourself, you will die in days. We are admitting you. You will need to eat every single thing we provide to you. If you do not, we will have to place a nasogastric tube in you, and you will receive all your nutrients from a tube."

All I heard through my eating disorder filter was, "Good job, Emily. You have lost so much weight! But we're all so fat that we will also need to make you fat, so we are going to be feeding you much more than necessary."

Everything were being brought to my bed by a nurse and a trained meal support worker. I actually had to eat the food being brought to me. Despite the fact that I had became good at hiding food, I couldn't hide food with two pairs of eyes watching my every move.

In the next two months at that hospital, I actually continued to lose weight (which I was ecstatic about at the time). This meant that my team at Victoria General Hospital had decided to send me over to BC Children's Inpatient Program. I was not okay with that decision. This meant more food, more rules, more weight gain.

The next month of waiting to get transferred to the worst place on earth, I spent my days crying. I had completely stopped talking to my parents or even allowing them in the same room with me. I was alone.

All this work, all this weight loss- it's just going to be thrown down the drain! "I am worthless. I am going to be even fatter. I cannot do this!" This was an every day thought that ran through my head, along with calories and calculations.

The day I made my way over to BC Children's Eating Disorder Unit, I left the harsh sterile conditions I had been living in for three months. No more measuring the input and output of my liquids, no more lying in a hospital bed 24/7, no being yelled at if I even sat up. Even with all those harsh rules, I was still not happy that I was leaving Victoria. By no means did I want to stay in Victoria but Vancouver sounded frightening, so unfamiliar. I saw it as a place of eating, eating, and even more eating. Eating six times a day, along with very strict rules. This place sounded like the worst situation that could happen to me.

It wasn't until I was admitted to BC Children's Eating Disorder Unit that I believed I was there. The next four months consisted of counting *calories, counting kilos, crying, eating, water loading, and learning new "anorexia tricks" from the other girls. Each week I gained two kilos. With each kilo came the torturous voice of my eating disorder: "You fat pig! You're worthless! Why don't you go die in a hole. No one would care if you did!" You are the most disgusting human being that has ever lived! This voice was an every day and every second narrative.*

I went on living like a robot on the outside, showing no emotion to others. A tornado of feelings and thoughts worked to destroy my mind and well being day after day. The only thing that was keeping me from becoming completely insane and giving up was the thought of getting out of that locked door prison and losing all the weight and more, I was going to be indestructible, I was going to show all these doctors, therapists, psychiatrists and especially my parents. To whom I was still not talking and whom I had no plan to start talking anytime soon.

During this time at BC Children's Hospital, I developed depression, anxiety, and I had started cutting. Cuts, scabs, and scars started to line my wrists all the way up my forearms. Gain weight: cut . Eat a meal or snack without hiding part of it: cut . My life was in a complete downward spiral! I was not showing it on the outside, so no one knew what was truly going on. So... I gained the weight and saw my freedom rapidly approaching. Four months after being admitted, I was released from the prison that had held kept me captive for what seemed like forever.

Finally back to eating no food: You worthless piece of crap, I thought when I first arrived at home. So that is what I did: NO FOOD, and lots and lots of exercising.

Sure enough, I lost the weight, one month later, I was back in Victoria General Hospital's Pediatrics Unit, but that time was different. I had a new approach. I was not going to eat anything, so the nurses would bring in the food, and I would refuse to eat it. They would sit, wait , expect me to give in, but there was no way! My eating disorder was stronger than ever, and was I ever proud of it! A couple of days went by, but no food passed my deteriorating lips.

Then in walked five nurses, two doctors and an anesthesiologist. I was about to be tubed, but I quickly decided that there was no way I was going to let them stick a tube in my nose, down my throat, and into my stomach.

I woke up to a portable x-ray leaving my room. I was in a hazy state. I tried pulling out the tube. No luck. The nurse was right there to stop me from pulling it out. She restrained me from undoing all the work the medical team had done. The tube was tearing up my throat. It probably was one of the most physically painful experiences I had ever endured. I could not talk, it hurt to breathe, and it was difficult to swallow anything. I was constantly sucking on ice chips to try and ease the pain. I endured this tube for approximately two weeks. It was finally removed because I was not able to tolerate the pain any longer. They took it out provided I promised to eat what they prepared, with the catch that if I didn't eat even one small part of the food, the tube would go back in.

A couple of months later, I was back in Vancouver in the eating disorders unit at BC Children's Hospital. For the first few days I skipped one meal a day, trying to keep my mind a bit calmer. I was then put on Intensive One-on-One Meal Support, where you would go into a room with one of the nurses. The food would then be brought in and placed in front of me. The nurse sat with you, eyes not leaving you for a moment. I would sit there for hours at a time until I ate all that was in front of me.

Then one day, it all changed I started to open up to a nurse. Andie was her name. Andie was my saving grace. She changed my life. She was the one who convinced me that indeed the grass is always greener on the other side. She herself was a recovered anorexic. She had suffered for many years, and I could relate to her immensely.

She would leave notes and inspirational sayings on little note cards and leave them on my night side table every night she worked. She kept me going. Before I got discharged she gave me her necklace that she had received while she was fighting her own battle, it is the eating disorder recovery sign. I could never repay her for the light and hope for freedom she brought into my life. I became determined to recover.

I began to eat all food provided to me, I gained my weight, I started to talk about my thoughts and feelings, and I began taking sertraline, an anti-depression pill that worked wonders. I am proud to say that I truly earned my final discharge from that BC Children's Hospital, the hospital that had truly been a rollercoaster of emotions and mind sets, the place where I had so many memories and so many new amazing, kind, and strong friends.

Here I am today still determined and committed to recovery and freedom from this demand. Every day I appreciate the many life lessons I have learned along this journey. The most important lesson I have learned as a result of my eating disorder is to live life to the fullest. I shall always remember what I have gone through and how strong I am.

I am a survivor."

Thank you for the stories.

I bless all of you who contributed, and shared your truth and hearts for the world! I love you awesome change makers!

I see each and every one of you. Your pain is something that another person has gone through. Or is feeling right this minute. That breath you just inhaled, should be a reminder of that- everyone of your breaths is a cycle to the same breaths everyone is inhaling at the same moment. We are all going through the struggle to stay standing.

Peace and love.

```
Stories leave

blueprints

on our souls
```

♡

LOVE YOUR SPIRIT
Twelve Spiritual Concepts
Taking you to the next level

One

I silence the world,

I press pause to whatever is happening in this moment,

This time, this feeling. Today is on hold,

And I breathe into that space where the world is put aside,

Where nothing else matters but my own nourishment and well-being;

And so, I silence my peers, I silence my parents, I silence my friends, I silence my teachers, I silence other voices;

And so, I listen to my OWN voice.

What do I hear?

I come inward, deepening a connection with myself, becoming increasingly in touch with my inner voice.

I hear the weeping and expression of my voice, the power of it, the creativity of it, the beauty of it.

I place my right palm over my heart.

What do I hear?

It's an urge to shout and scream: "I am here!"

What do you hear?

Tune inward. Feel your breath rising and falling.

It could be a wordless cry within you, waiting patiently to come out from hiding.

There are no words to catch this feeling.

And so, I tap into my own beating heart. I hear its beat, beat after beat uplifting my spirit, like music entering my eardrums, and loving my soul.

And so, this moment I hear my own voice being heard. For once and for all, I hear it.

The world is your waiting game.

The world is silent; the world is on pause.

When the time is right, I'll press *play* to hear the world.

I find balance between listening to others and myself,

Pausing when I need nourishment,

Playing when I need wisdom.

♡

You may be driven to continue this journey of spiritual concepts that changed my life. Nothing is stopping you.

Feel your spirit come alive.

Two

I inhale and exhale,

I inhale and exhale.

I notice the thoughts.

They come and go.

I do not pay attention to each individual thought.

I let my thoughts play like a movie,
showing me scene by scene.

I let them unravel like a story,
showing me chapter after chapter.

And so I stare right into the chapters of my thoughts,
looking from a higher perspective,

Almost as if I am on top of the world,
looking down to one thought after the next,

One sadder than the next, one happier than the next.
One is a memory, one a future dream, one a fantasy.

The amazing spiritual teacher, Eckhart Tolle, says:
"This, too, will pass."

Thoughts will come, heartbreaks will happen,
but "they, too, will pass".

Life will pass, like a breath coming and going,

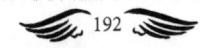

one deeper than the next.

I inhale and exhale,

inhale and exhale,

And feel my breath rising and falling.

I see my thoughts coming and going.

And that too, is how you should live your life.

Watch them come, watch them leave.

Meditation is not about getting into a state of
completeness, with no thoughts at all.
Where's the pleasure in that?
It's about the stories that arise.

Soak up a connection with your sweet soul,
and see what happens when you let go of the grip
you've been holding so tightly on life.

Three

One of my favorite spiritual teachers once said:
"There are no extra pieces in the universe. Everyone is here because he or she has a place to fill, and every piece must fit itself into the big jigsaw puzzle."
Deepak Chopra

Purpose is the word that is engraved in all our hearts.

We all have purpose.

But does everyone know his or her purpose?

The person who walked by me in the grocery store today has a reason to be here on earth.
She has purpose,
Whether or not she realizes it.
She has a reason to be alive,
Whether or not she understands.
She has a duty to do.
The universe brought her here to do something:
To make a difference,
or to make chaos in somebody's life.
She is to bring light into lives
or bring darkness into lives,

And so, just like Deepak said: "There are no extra pieces". There are not too many people. Everyone has a role to play.

What's your purpose?

Four

Guidance.

It's a word that frightens us.

All of us always wanting to do everything on our own,

To hustle and bustle, to work so hard we end up sick,

All to show people that I can do this;
I am independent,

And so we never ask for help,

The universe helps those who trust in the source.

The universe helps those who do NOT feel ashamed
to ask for assistance.

The universe asks those who can say:
"Please help me find self confidence,
please bring me to the right people,
please give me help to finish this album
or to finish this book,
please help me… "

In asking for help,

We become lighter,

as if we are falling,

falling free.

Five

Every morning I connect with my spirit.

I come inwards,

Listening to that inner voice once again.

It's my soul,
it's my precious spirit wanting to come out and play.

And so I let it out.

I place my right palm over my heart.

I tell myself: "You are beautiful Brittany.
You have a beautiful figure."

I connect with my heart centre,
and because my heart has felt unworthy before,

I keep reminding her how beautiful she is,

Letting the positive words set the intention for the day.

I feel pulse after pulse,

beat after beat.

I am alive.

Six

Yang to my yin,
Male to my female,
I am a soul in a human body.
There's a balance of energy in me.

They say there should be
half masculine and half feminine,
But that is not always the case.

However, there is dark to my light,
good to my bad, rain to my sunshine,
depression to my joy.

And so, understanding when Yang – Male, dark,
intense, driven, devoted, hardworking, focused – and
Yin – Female, light, happy, joyful, dreamy, sunny –
come together,
it becomes a union of oneness.

I take one breath, reminding myself that there will
always be half and half,

Good and bad.

And so, understanding this concept,
I live fully in the now, knowing what to expect,

Acknowledging that there is a light
at the end of the tunnel.

There has to be: No light without darkness.
Be the Yin to your Yang.

Seven

Energy.
It's in all of us.
It's in me. It's in you. It's in your phone.
It's in my yoga teacher. It's in my mother.
We are all energy.

We all have an aura around us.

There's a frequency around you.
It vibrates with other frequencies.
That's why you "vibe" well with one person
and not the other.
You are tapping into
their energy, and yours.

Be mindful of whose energy is around you.

Some is positive, some negative.
You might become drained and sucked
into a negative person's energy.

You're a sensitive soul,
and so people take advantage of you,
and drag you into their hurt, their pain, their bullshit.

Protect yourself.
Your energy is precious.
It's beautiful. It's innocent.
Some people like to corrupt.
Don't pay attention to them,

Because energy demands attention.

Eight

Clear your energy.

Take deep breaths.

Get rid of those energies that do not belong to you.

I breathe into the space for my soul.

In the sky my energy is renewed.

Into the earth my old energy goes.

I inhale and create fresh energy from the sky.

I exhale and release negativity into the earth.

I breathe in.

I breathe out.

I breathe in.

I breathe out.

I am revived.

Nine

I see myself as I see others.

We all reflect each other.

I used to dislike looking into people's eyes,
letting them see the depth of my soul.

Now

I look deeply into people's eyes.

I see through them;

I see myself.

I see a reflection,

A mirror image.

I see you in me, me in you.

I see the bad in others as the same bad in me,

I see the good in others as the same good in me.

You reflect me.

I reflect you.

Ten

My precious spirit is within me. It's there,

Deepak Chopra, *The Deeper Wound*:
"When you breathe gently and slowly, the body relaxes, the mind finds its still center, and the stage is set for inspiration—the flowing in of spirit."

He speaks to my spirit.

As I take one slow breath, I feel myself letting go and becoming more centered in Now.

As I take another breath, I feel myself becoming connected with my spirit, letting it flow freely.

As I take another breath, I feel myself becoming connected to this sacred moment, to the divine.

And so, this moment, my soul is with me,
Comforting me, and loving me for who I am.

The *Prana* (life force) is activated.
My breath is my life force. I give it thanks.

Once I had pneumonia. I had to stay in bed for two months. My breath was shallow. It was hard to breathe. I feared my lungs would stop.
But they didn't, and I learned.

Every time I inhale and exhale, I am thankful.

I'm alive.

Eleven

Shadow self, come forward. Show me yourself.

Merge with me, unfold who you are.

Let me see who I really am.

My shadow self is dark.

I push it aside.

I hide it under a mask of lies,

And layers of grief and sadness.

The shadow self has protected me, kept me alive.

So I won't repress it. I will ask it to come forward.

And I will heal its wound,

Naturally and organically.

And then

I will release it.

Twelve

They tell me:
"Women are like a lotus, growing from within.
The flower transforms from the root of darkness."

Woman becomes her true divinity
as her petals blossom.

Yang to her yin,

Her natural seed, to give life to her petals.

To become a true lotus,

She needs to put aside what the world
wants her to be.

She needs to put aside jealousy
towards other women.

She needs to put aside negative thoughts
about her body.

No more expectations.

She needs to put aside her ego.

No more flight or fight.

As she blossoms,
She finds her strength;
She finds her centre;
She finds love for herself.

It's her walk, not his.

He may come and go, but she stays.

Sometimes it hurts her,
and sometimes being sensitive feels like a burden.

But not anymore.

She knows that is her strength, her power.

For every time she has fallen to the ground in pain,
and cried up to the universe:
"I can't do this anymore,"
she has earned a great understanding.

Now she knows she can.
She has blossomed.
She is a lotus.

Never forget your power.
It's in you.

Kundalini energy:
Power that starts from our spine
and rises upwards to our heart.

A woman is a powerful thing.

I hope you felt driven to deepen your knowledge a bit more. Don't forget: "Spirituality" is nothing "weird". It's simply your belief and how you live your life. Spirituality is about the spirit within you that wants to come out and play.

I hope you feel awakened.

Love and light.

Britt

♡

CHAPTER EIGHTEEN
Being Average Sucks

Who said being different is a bad thing?

Society says: You need to go to university and get a degree. You need to hang out with the cool people in order to be accepted.

Our peers say: You need to dress the same as everyone else. You need to gossip and hurt others.

That's not fair. Of course it's not fair.

There's this boy I know. He isn't your average kid. He wears pink nail polish. He wears girls' clothing sometimes. He hears what they call him at school: "Gay. Loser. Fag. Stupid. Worthless." He hears those words every day.

But it doesn't beat him down. It doesn't defeat him. Like I said, he's not your average teen. He embraces who he is. He wears whatever he wants. When people laugh, he laughs back.

When he leaves school, he lives a life he has chosen. He's not like most teens, who go home not knowing who they are.

It's okay to be different. It's okay to wear pink nail polish. It's okay to like the opposite sex or the same sex. It's okay to meditate every morning. It's okay to believe in spirituality. It's okay to have your whole body covered in tattoos, if that's what you want to do. It's okay to be YOU.

I remember saying to my mom: "I embrace being an outcast. The greatest thing I can do is to talk to all kinds of 'losers' at my school. To be someone who isn't part of the popular group anymore is awesome."

Embrace being different. Try being an outcast from time to time.

I still suffer about fitting in. I always feel different. Maybe that's my own insecurity. Or maybe I actually am different. Who cares?

There will always be people who hate. There will always be rude comments. The trick is, you can choose to react or not to react.

It's too boring to wear the same clothes as everyone else, or speak the same, look the same, to be the same.

As much as some of us dedicate our lives trying to be average, we're all unique. So it's silly to change our clothes, to build masks and covers just so we can feel as though we fit in – to be called "average".

Because guess what? Wake up! Being average is BORING.

You're are different. You are you. Embrace that. Celebrate it.

I'm not your average teen.

And that's okay.

#WhoWants2BeAverage? #WhenYouCanBeDifferent

Have you ever felt like being difference is a bad thing? Tell me about it. What makes you different? Whatever that is… Only makes you an extraordinary person.

Dear older Brittany,

I see your pain. I notice it. I feel your teardrops. I feel your throat closing because of how afraid you were to speak.

That's the old you.

I see who you've become. I feel your strength. I feel your heart blossoming with giggles and happiness. And damn am I a very proud older version of yourself.

Thank you for not giving up on yourself. You've kept fighting, you had gotten the opportunity to see beautiful places, see more snowflakes, and meet great people- also, meet assholes. Life gave you a ticket to keep going, and you took it.

I am proud of you.

The new me.

Message From My Mentors

"When I met Britt she was so on fire. It was contagious. Like an all consuming flame that lit up any room she was in. I knew right away that this young woman was here on purpose. She's a force to be reckon with. This girl is on fire. Far beyond her years. She is a such an old soul."
-Tyler Nicholson, Youth Adviser & Mentor.

"When I first met Brittany she was a shy, awkward, 16 year old, unsure of her beauty, strength and power. Now...wow! She has grown and continues to grow everyday into a her depth, clarity, power and wisdom - with the courage to share herself openly with the world. She has assumed a powerful leadership position for those who need her voice more than anyone - our Youth! Bravo young Brittany! Keep up the great work!"
-Emily E. Cleland, Spiritual Guide & Mentor

"Brittany has evolved considerably over the last few months, her understanding of her souls quality has grown and her desire to share her wisdom with others has exponentially increased as a result of this new found confidence. It's a pleasure observing the likes of this woman transform into the butterfly that she is!"
-Noreen Kassam, Spiritual Adviser & founder of Selena Moon Project.

"The opportunity to be a witness to 'another's becoming' is a 'sacred thing'. I've watched Britt bravely invite us into her own transformation. She uses writing as her medium. She relates to the struggle of adolescence with the mind, spirit and voice of woman wise beyond her years."
-Cori Calkins, Psychologist & College Division Manager at Ian Sommerhalder Foundation.

"Brittany's transformation has been unbelievable! She went from a shy young girl to an empowered strong female who is committed to helping others to see their light. She is truly a beautiful example of how one can feel so sad and alone their entire life, too then awaken to the possibilities of helping others, and becoming truly fulfilled and ALIVE with that."
-Judy Machado-Duque, author of "Life Purpose Playbook."

Dear All My Readers

Wherever you are in life, I hope my words gave you comfort, or realization of who you really are.

Maybe this journey has given you the chance to discover your worth. Maybe this journey has given you the chance to know who you really are, despite what others tell you. Maybe this journey has given you a chance to change your lifestyle, from negative to positive. Maybe my words gave you a flicker of hope to keep fighting challenging days. Maybe my words gave you comfort in one of your darkest nights.

Or perhaps my story just gave you the opportunity to escape from your reality.

Someone once told me, "Britt, remember this: Life is like music". I kept thinking, "How can you compare life to music?" Until the answer finally showed up.

Music has its highs and lows, life has its ups and downs. Its fast pace. And it's slow melodies.

Like music, like is dramatic, beautiful, yet very frightening. There are always going to be highs and lows: heartbreaks and victories, losing and gaining friends, teary nights and joyful days. And everything in between. But that is life for you, we change, expand and evolve into who we really are within time from falling a little bit. Wherever you go in life, please read this book as many times as you wish: and know I am really just a book away, and will always be there for you.

I don't know about you but I plan on spending the rest of my life going with the flow: riding the waves instead of against the tide. And making beautiful music, not the kind we listen too; the kind we experience, from high and low melodies.

This is the way I choose to live my life. That I promise you.

Brittany Krystantos

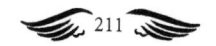

Acknowledgments

These people have inspired me. They have uplifted me with their positive energy. They have helped me become the writer I'm meant to me. These are the people who gave me support, cheering me on the sideline. It's a long list.

To my family
With immense love and gratitude, I thank my parents, **Mandy and Mitchell**, who have launched me on this journey and who support me unconditionally. Thank you for having the trust in me to know that whatever I do I will be led to the right path. Thank you for giving me the freedom to do transitional schooling rather than finishing my last year of high school. Thank you for giving me the freedom to go to Bali in the summer, and for letting me go to the places I need to go to make my dreams come true.

To the rest of my family: Sister **Samantha, Bubbies, Zaidas, Grandpa, Aunts, Uncles** and **Cousins**, I want you to know that each of you has played an important part in helping me along this path. I love you all very much.

To my supporters
The people who contributed to making this book possible

To my editor, **Francie Healy**, thank you for working incredibly hard to bring my voice through text and allowing it to shine. You're an inspiration to this book itself. You taught me the greatest lesson of all – paying it forward. You told me to pay it forward to a charity in trade for your services. I plan on doing exactly that. You saw something in my writing. You told me I'm a born writer. Thank you for believing in me and in my work. This writing journey doesn't end here.

To **Ivana Carlosena**, my front and back cover is beautifully designed because of your hard work and understanding of the vision for my book. You came into my life from the time I didn't speak. You watched me blossom into the girl who has now formed her voice. This book wouldn't be possible without your God-given talents. Thank you.

Theresa McNeilly, this book REALLY wouldn't be possible without your designs and formatting. You understood my book as if it were yours, and you got to know who I am, which shows in your design. You brought beautiful energy into this book. You have one true God-given talent!

ACKNOWLEDGMENTS

Thank you.

Elizabeth Woods, you told me: "Let's do this together and show the world what you have to say." Thank you for staying true to your promise, and for being such a guiding light, for giving me the platform to speak my truth. I couldn't have asked anyone else to market this. Your energy gives warmth and infinite love to everyone you meet.

Felipe Gabriele, thank you for creating my website and putting such positive energy into it. I saw your other work and knew instinctively that you were the right person to make my website. Thank you!

To my mentors
The people who helped heal me and who kept my soul nourished with love

T'ameaux Brown, where do I start? Let's backtrack a bit. I found you while I was in the dark. I was stuck in a tunnel, hoping to find the light, hoping that with guidance and support I might be able to crawl through that frightening place and reach for the light. I felt as though I was gasping for air. "Let me get through this universe," I said. "Show me the light!"

And you, T'ameaux, came. You came with your beautiful soul, hugging me into your embrace, holding me tight, reminding me that I would get through this. "One breath at a time," you said. "This shall pass." Your light kept me going. When I fell and truly needed you, I received a text message from you, once again reminding me that divine timing does exist. You have not just helped my emotional state and spiritual wellbeing. You have made this book possible. How? I did write it all myself. You might be wondering how you contributed. I'll tell you how. You were the one who said: "Buy a journal; grab a pen; and start expressing your feelings, morning and night." Just that made me realize that writing isn't just my form of healing but my joy, my passion. I started to love mornings and nights. I started to reach closer to the light... and closer still... until I realized there wasn't much darkness anymore, that I had finally reached it.

You, "Healer T", are a blessing. You are my soul sister. You are a true reflection that every woman is like a lotus; that we grow from the roots of darkness; and once our petals have blossomed, our light is bright. I love you forever and always. Thank you for bringing my gifts and talents out. It is my greatest wish to take every lesson, gift and piece of knowledge that you have given me and pass them to every person I encounter so they can be blessed with the same gifts. I love you, Healer T!

Prasad Paul Duffy, you are a true blessing. You are a gift to this world. You showed up in my life one day and I knew I needed to message you. I knew that I could learn a lot from your teaching. We "Skyped" and within a few minutes I was smiling. Your energy lifted me up just like that. My aura became lighter. Most of my mentors are women, but you've become the first male spiritual guru and adviser who has made me feel comfortable. I didn't worry or get tense with you. You tuned into my energy and connected me with my true essence, my true being, my pure light. You reminded me of my purpose. You reminded me of my future. You reminded me that my intuition is that feeling in the centre of my being, and never to stop listening to it. You reminded me that I still need to find similar souls, that I still need to connect with people who understand me on a vibrational level. You reminded me that there are other people like me, people who are creators and writers, who will give me the hope that "I shall live in divine flow". You reminded me that when the time comes, I'll meet them.

Serena Dyer, I messaged you when I was 15. I had a clear idea of what I wanted to do in this lifetime, but I didn't have the confidence to do it. I told you I wanted to help others, that writing was my passion, my joy; that I wanted to use it as a platform to help others. You encouraged me to keep writing, and never to abandon my thoughts because they were special. You told me to start writing and not to delete any of it. I used to throw it away because I felt what I was writing wasn't good enough. You said the best thing anyone can do is to shine brightly, without caring if anyone notices. You said this alone helps liberate others from their fears. Your words continue to give me encouragement. There are moments of doubt, of course, but motivation from someone who has "done it" always helps. Thank you.

Cori Calkins, we had a special bond from the first email you sent me. Thank you for taking your time to sit with me over Skype and to go through each chapter with me to make sure I'm not forgetting any important things to mention. You've not just become my mentor but my friend too. Thank you for getting me through my difficult and transitional time. You rock! I love you!

Emily Cleland, thank you for your guidance. I'll never forget your treatment that has given me hope and clarity. Because of it, I am who I am today: stronger, wiser, and happier. I love you!

Noreen, thank you for sharing your beautiful story in this book. You are that woman who always inspires me to feel beautiful and confident in my own skin. Your support and unconditional has helped shape me into who I am today. I love you, beautiful soul sista!

TO MY POSITIVE FRIENDS AND INSPIRATIONS
My yoga community

Anna, thank you for being like a sister, mentor, friend and cheerleader all in one. I will always remember one day as if it were yesterday. I was lying head downwards in your massage bed. You said, "How about trying Yoga? Go to a Moksha studio. You'll fall in love with the community." A few days earlier, someone had actually given me a Moksha Maple free pass so I could try it out. Your words were a sign from the universe that I was meant to land in a Moksha studio. Anna, you are my rock and my strength at times where I need it. You always remind me to keep aiming forward. Let's not forget your advice when I had formed a crush on one of my classmates (I was maybe 14). You told me to bump into him in the hallway and push his books to the floor, say "Hey!" and then wink. You bring out the little goddess within me that just wants to play and enjoy life. I keep thanking you for introducing me to Yoga, and more importantly, to Moksha Yoga. You answer: "No, my love; it wasn't me. You would have found Yoga on your own. I just helped you get there sooner." Well, thank you for that. I love you tons!

Moksha Yoga Thornhill, you've become my home in such a time of need. You've become my healing space, where I inhaled love and exhaled gratitude. You've become my family, where bonds were made, teachers were my mentors and friends, and the community became my home. Tears well up in my eyes thinking about the transition I've made in this time period of practicing in your space. The discovery happened when I realized that I want to be a Yoga Teacher, too. I remember walking into the heated room and I could envision myself walking into that same room a few years later, teaching and doing what I love: to help others. I discovered that Yoga is not just the Asanas. I recall hearing Elliot say: "We are NOT the poses. We are the breath and the feelings that arise." *Magic happened in this space.*

Darcy, thank you for creating such a beautiful space, and thank you for welcoming me with open arms. I remember the moment I first stepped into your studio. I stopped for a moment and gasped. And I thought to myself, "This is my home." I may have not started here in the beginning of my Yoga journey, but along my "becoming" and my discovery, I found you guys. I am certain there will be more healing moments taking place here. I love you, soul sister!

Carmelinda Dimanno, I met you two years ago at Moksha Maple. I barely knew you. I stuck to my night classes, following a steady routine – 8 pm classes and that was it. We didn't cross paths very much until I walked into your Yoga Barre class during my first class at Moksha Yoga Thornhill. Ever since that moment, we've shared such a sacred bond and friendship. Someone once asked me: "If you could be one woman, who would that be?" Many women might say, "A Victoria's Secret model." But no. I thought, if I could be anyone, it would be you, Carm. You're a beautiful goddess who cares for people, who teaches from your heart, who follows your passion, who is powerful and strong. Even in grief, you breathe through it. I ask myself how I can be like you. I don't mean become a copy of you, but how can I find your positive qualities in myself? I remember coming to your event, where we danced even though something tragic had happened that day. I found out someone I loved was falsely diagnosed with cancer. You looked at me. There were tears in my eyes and you said: "You showed up. That shows lots of strength. You probably would rather be home right now moping and crying. But you're here." The first day I walked into the Thornhill studio, you gave me a big hug, even though you didn't know me well. You welcomed me into this community, this space as if to say: "This is your home now." I will never forget the morning I came out of your class all sweaty; crying, because this class FINALLY brought feelings into my body- and allowed me to process some emotional triggers. I ran to you. I took one look at you, and cried and not pretty tears- it was a full out bawling and gasping; ugly cry. I ran into your arms, and rest my head on your shoulder, while I heavily cried; you held me and told me "everything will be okay." You provide such a safe haven, and it felt nice to just let it all out, not being afraid of being seen in my most vulnerable state, and crying for help for once, not holding it in, it felt good to let someone in, especially because I trust you more then anyone I know. You told me: "tears doesn't make a woman weak, it makes her strong." I really believe that now. You girl, are something special. You offer a mommy energy for other women, you're a soul sister for so many women, we look up to you for advice; thank you for being all that for me. I love you so much!

Paria Mirazimi! Damn, girl! Words can't express the love I have for you. You've watched me grow. You've seen me at my worst. We've shared lots of sweat, love and tears. I remember the first time I took your class. It was at Moksha Yoga Maple, and you were such a natural at teaching, talking, transforming the entire room, that I fell in love with the Asana practice. You were the one who made me want to be a teacher myself. You walked with confidence into that room. And despite how you felt, despite what life had thrown you – challenges, defeats, happiness and accomplishments, it was always about your students, never yourself. You said the room and your students' mats are their healing journeys. You said your problems had to be left outside the room at all times. These are words I will never forget. I am so honored to have an entire chapter by you. There are a lot of mentors and instructors I look up to, but I couldn't ask anyone better to write the Yoga chapter. Tuesday was our night to sweat and leave as better versions of ourselves. I love you, girl!

Oh, **Elliott**! Thank you for teaching me more in your classes than anything I've learned in a self-help book. It's true. You've taught me the most important thing about Yoga. You say, We are not the poses but the moment to moment. When you told me I inspired you, I was shocked for a minute. My eyes got a little watery. I thought, how the heck could I inspire such a strong, powerful, beautiful soul like Elliott? Truth is, you inspire *me* to be better, to be stronger, to smile more often, to enjoy life, to laugh more (I don't do enough) and to live with joy. Our bond is so special, almost as if we understand each other on a soul level. One time after class, I was complaining in a whiny voice: "Elliott! That was hard! I kept falling!" You stopped me and you said: "But you did it, didn't you? I did it on purpose. You can get too comfortable in your classes. I knew you needed a little bit of challenge – something your body wasn't used to." Well, thank you for that, Elliott! You bring so much joy and inspiration into everyone's lives. When the time comes, we are writing a book together! I love you! Thanks for being the soul brother that I have never had.

Sara Salehi, you make me want to just dance and be crazy. You make me want to laugh and let everything out. I don't think there is even one class of yours where I didn't laugh and have fun. You bring such a fun energy into your classes. I won't forget the time I had a HEALING moment in your class: I recall leaving the class halfway through, and swearing to myself about how "I am not capable of Yoga or anything." You haven't forgotten that moment. It's pretty funny. It makes me laugh just thinking about it now.

Stephanie Mills: Girl, you're such a blessing. Let's not forget the time I was getting anxious about finding a job, so you took some of your free time to sit with me, talk over a cup of tea, and name all the feelings I shouldn't be afraid of. Thank you so much for your support. I knew I could always come to you. You've inspired me to be the kind of teacher who will always make time for my students. I love you!

Thank you to the rest of my **Moksha Yoga Community**. You have all been such a big contributor to who I am now!

To the rest of my positive tribe

Ryan Savien, thank you for being my voice when I didn't have one. You're the little boy in chapter one, the one who spoke for me when I couldn't. You told the teacher I was hungry, or needed to use the washroom. You inspired me to speak. You gave me the confidence to speak. You showed me I was never really alone. I love you, Ry. Thank you for being my voice.

Carmelia Ray, thank you for saying to me a few years ago: "We need to get you a blog. You're a born writer." Thank for launching my website. And for giving me the opportunity to write my heart and soul! I love you!

Des, thank you for always listening to my long vents about how *"he is such a jerk"*. You've inspired me to always speak my truth, and live by it. Our friendship is beyond special and your love, support and friendship got me through some rocky roads. I love you, soul sister!

Aunty Robin, thank you for teaching me everything I need to know about how to play the game right – about what to do when you see a cute boy. And don't worry, I'll never forget our pool chills in Vegas, when I was the student and you were the teacher, educating me on Bananas. I wasn't going to mention names, because you know how our family will get. I'll hear: "Why didn't you name me?" or "Why did you name her and not me?" Well... Who cares? I make the rules. I'll name whomever I want. You're my friend, my sister – not just my aunt. I love you. Thank you for everything you do for me.

Bubbie Kim, thank you so much for being here for me throughout this journey. What can I say? We are so similar. We share similar beliefs, struggles; and I love the sisterly bond we share! You've given me the greatest gift of all, encouraging me to write this book. I love you!

Jodi Milunsky, thank you for sitting with me during our free time on lunch break, in my eleventh grade; going through my chapters, giving your opinion, even when you should have been doing homework. Instead, you always took your time to help me with your most wonderful ideas. You are a true writer. You have it within you. Thank you!

Aunty Veronica, or should I say Aunty Kaka – Thank you for your support, your love, and your advice. We've been on this walk together for a while now. We used to bump heads – never understood each other. Maybe that's because deep down we are basically the same, act the same, react the same, like twin flames! I'm glad we've come to see eye to eye with each other. I love you, soul sister! Thank you for all your support!

Bubbie Jojo, thank you for staying up all night with me writing and expanding my creativity. We had fun sleepovers, fun chats about boys. Thank you. I love you!

Meital, you're the girl I mentioned twice in this book, the girl I disliked in grade four, because I didn't give you a chance to show me how great you are; and you're the girl who became my best friend when I had lost my spot at the "popular" table. You sat with me in the hallway of second floor, away from "popular" judgmental brats. This one time, we both said: "I love being an outcast." Thank you for getting me through high school! I love you, girl!

Zaida Lorrie, thank you for picking me up whenever I call you, taking me places an hour or more away, believing in me, and being the male figure I've always needed to keep me strong and motivated. Thank you for everything you've done for me. Also, I'll never forget the cookies you make to cheer my mood! You're the one man who has never failed me, and that is something I take seriously, since lots have failed me. You remind me that not all men are bad, and there are good ones – that one day I'll find him. I love you so much. I really don't know how I could survive without you.

And to me: I place my hand over my heart, feel it beat, and think: I need to take a moment to thank myself. Thank you, Britt. For not giving up. For being one of those teens who pushed past obstacles as if it was the easiest thing to do. You're the reason this book is possible. You're the reason your life means something.

ABOUT THE AUTHOR

Brittany Krystantos is a 18-year-old girl that grew up thinking being different was a bad thing, while she saw the world between her eyes – literally. She lived silently for the first seven years of her life, dealing with the world's efforts to bring her down to their level of insecurity, an experience that heavily shaped her life. When high school came along, she struggled silently, never telling anybody the bad thoughts that would find their way to her at night. It got so bad, it was make it or break it – change her life around or dwell in the negativity that consumed her life. She made a promise to herself: get up from the funk, smile more, laugh more, and get ready to rock this world. This change helped enable and build her positive tribe of people to lean on, especially her mentor, who came running into Britt's life when she needed her the most. Britt understood the very important lesson that typically takes people years to discover: she's never really alone.

Positivity became her quest.

One day she discovered writing is a part of her soul. It was in her birthright; she just needed the push to find this knowledge for herself. Her mentor said, "Grab a journal. Get a pen. Write how you feel every day."

Writing once was an outlet to vent, then became a place for others to soak up inspiration. Britt loves writing positive inspiration, but don't underestimate her – she loves writing sexy romances during her free time when she is not trying to inspire others, doing yoga, drinking green tea, or lifting weights at the gym to feel more badass then she already is.

Brittany loves to hear from her readers. Visit her website at: www.brittkrystantos.com You can also find her on Facebook (Britt Krystantos) or Twitter (@Brittkrystantos).

Made in the USA
Middletown, DE
30 April 2016